Empower your people to
achieve the extraordinary

BY DAVE STITT

ISBN: 978-0-9567747-2-9

Editor: Rod Sweet
Illustrations: Gary Nightingale
Covers and design: David Prendergast

About the Author

Dave Stitt has been coaching executive teams in the construction industry for more than two decades. Before that, as a civil engineer, he rose to senior management positions in national construction and engineering firms. He has raced in over a hundred triathlons, winning several, and represented Great Britain in the 1991 Triathlon World Championship in Australia. He and wife Sue have two creative sons and live in Washington in the north east of England. He is co-author of *21st Century People Leadership,* and author of *We Need to Talk about Collaboration* and *Deep and Deliberate Delegation: A New Art for Unleashing Talent and Winning Back Time.*

CONTENTS

Part 3: Changing the Industry From the Ground Up

Industry reaction to the Coach for Results course

'I would recommend you consider this short and practical online course if you work in construction and want to develop your own or your key team members' management style. Much of what I talk about related to industry modernisation is focused on the need for technology adoption, a move towards modern methods of construction and future skills.

'At the heart of enabling this to happen, though, is the need to have people in positions of influence able to coach, mentor, embed innovation, drive organisational performance and to act as a magnet for new talent into the industry. Dave Stitt PCC has a wealth of hard-earned experience from site to boardroom to share here in driving bottom-up change.'

– *Mark Farmer, Author of "Modernise or die" and founding director & CEO at Cast*

'This is a super initiative and I can envisage significant interest and engagement from young professionals and others seeking to hone their management and collaboration skills for the benefit of the construction industry around the world.

'The advent of the pandemic and climate change/carbon neutral initiatives have increased the need for collaborative, solution driven, problem solving skillsets. Bravo!'

– Chris Soffe PPCIOB FRICS FAIC MCIArb. MCMI CEnv; Non Executive Director, Global Supervisory Board at Gleeds, Vice Chairman Gleeds Americas

'Dave and his team are delivering a brilliant programme; it's a serious play to generate sustainable change that the construction industry needs. Not only that, it's taught by a true leadership coach at the top of his game! I know this because I've been lucky enough to have Dave spend some of his time coaching me, providing incredible insight and enhancing my performance on so many levels. Needless to say, I'd highly recommend Dave and the programme!'

– David Stephenson BEng (Hons) MBA ChPP CMgr MAPM MCMI, Project Manager at WSP in the UK

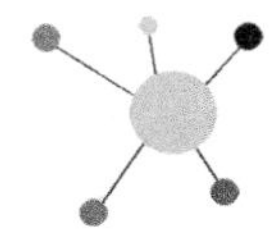

Introduction: We can adapt

For the last two decades I've been coaching construction company boards and teams in charge of some of the biggest projects in the UK. I started doing this after leading an award-winning culture-change programme at Wates. (For two decades before that, I was on the sharp end of delivering projects for national contractors.)

In recent years, it dawned on me that the coaching techniques I apply in my work with construction business leaders could, and should, be used by those leaders themselves in their dealings with each other, and by people in management roles all throughout the industry. The techniques are easy for anyone to use, and they make a big difference in fostering trust, enthusiasm and teamwork, and in growing people's confidence and capability, something construction really needs.

Toward that end, I developed a course for construction

professionals, called Coach for Results, on how to incorporate these techniques into their management styles.[1] In essence, a coaching style of management is one where you move away from giving orders and hunting for non-compliance – which is termed a 'command-and-control' style of management – and you put your people in charge of fulfilling their accountabilities while supporting them in finding their own way to do that. Basic coaching techniques give managers who have no intrinsic gift for or formal training in people management simple tools for bringing out the best in their people so great results can be achieved.

I mean no disrespect to experienced managers in construction. They have amassed huge personal knowledge, experience, authority and influence, and all of that naturally lends itself to telling people what to do. It can seem to be the easiest thing to do all round, and it is very satisfying, knowing and advising and helping. However, it is a trap because when you help someone you make them helpless. When you give orders and instructions, the people you are ordering and instructing stop thinking for themselves. Managers I coach often complain that they're 'the only one doing the thinking around here'. I complained of the same thing when I was a command-and-control project manager. That's what happens with command-and-control. With coaching, experienced managers don't disown their

---

[1] Details of the course can be found here: https://dsabuilding.co.uk/#coach4results

expertise, they give others the chance to become expert as well, so they're not so lonely at the top.

Think of it as a bit of social technology – an 'app', if you like – a new protocol guiding how we are with each other. In my view, construction's social technology is outdated. It has not kept up with changes in other types of technology and in society at large. As I'll show, I believe this is the root cause of the industry's chronic problems of poor quality, low productivity and its struggles to attract talent. The industry's fragmented and adversarial nature is often blamed for these problems, and for good reason, but none of us can change the way the industry is structured; it evolved that way, pushed by forces beyond our control, and it is what it is. We can, however, change the way we are with each other in our teams, business units and companies. We can adapt so that our team, business unit or company is having a better time, with less stress and conflict, while achieving consistently good results and enjoying the competitive advantage that brings.

As a social technology 'app', a coaching style of management is not like the big, top-down culture-change programmes I led from the late 1990s. These were fascinating and worthwhile but, in hindsight, they were also disruptive, resource-hungry, uncertain and took years to bear fruit. In contrast, a coaching style of management can start right now in any pocket of your business and, with a little encouragement, it can spread organically so that culture change happens quite swiftly with minimal disruption, cost and uncertainty.

There are three parts to this book. Because the idea of a coaching management style is new to construction, Part 1 sets out the basics of what the coaching style of management is, why construction companies need it, and the basic psychological underpinnings of why it works. Part 2 sets out how to do it. Part 3 explores how a coaching management culture can take root and change the industry from the ground up.

I hope you find it useful.

PART ONE

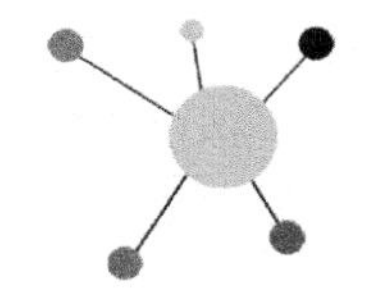

The What and Why

CHAPTER 1

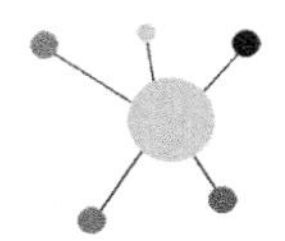

The prism of potential: What a coaching approach to management is

Each of us comes to work with huge potential and we want to do our best. We're valuable storehouses of energy, skills and talents, ready to be harnessed. Coaching starts with this premise, and the coach initiates an ongoing dialogue with the person being coached, the goal being to raise their awareness of their potential and to think afresh about how to fulfil it. Through coaching, a person is empowered to move themselves forward from where they are now to where they want to be, articulating the goals they want to achieve and overcoming the barriers they face.

Managers can be coaches. In fact, as we'll see, they should be. With coaching, you do two important things. First, you shift your focus away from your colleague's current performance and you begin to focus on their potential. When you do this you stop seeing them as a problem to be fixed and you start seeing them as a treasure to be discovered.

Second, you offer yourself to be a partner in a joint endeavour between the two of you, the purpose of which is to generate new, productive thinking on their part about their potential and how to meet it. Often we don't think very clearly about our potential, especially if we're given to believe that we don't have much of it.

The way you encourage new, productive thinking on their part is through a particular type of conversation that we call the coaching conversation. You initiate and manage this conversation, and the second part of this book is about how to do that. There is nothing technically difficult about initiating and managing a coaching conversation; it's simple, just not something most of us do because we've never thought about it before. With practice, it will become second nature.

As the manager, you initiate the coaching conversation with an invitation: you say, 'What do you think?', and then you listen. This invitation radically alters the dynamic between you and them. For starters, you're making yourself available to the other person in a way you may never have done before. You're offering your time and attention. It also signals that you value them and are interested in what they're thinking and have to say. It creates a safe space in which they are empowered to think and map their own way forward so that they can own their accountabilities more fully. That's why we're going to call you the coach and them 'the thinker'. You will be creating the space for them to do their own thinking and their own work.

Coaching is the opposite of the old management style I absorbed when I entered the industry in 1976. This management style is mostly blind to people's potential and focusses instead on performance or, more specifically, how closely people follow orders (compliance). It uses external enticements like cash and promotion to reward good performance, and negative responses like anger, blame and demotion to punish bad performance. I championed this style and rose up through the ranks by being aggressive, shouty and intimidating because it seemed to be expected of me, and when once I saw 'Dave Stitt is a bastard!' scrawled on the wall of a portable toilet, I was proud. (I'd be mortified today.)

As we'll see, these 'extrinsic' motivators as they're called – because they come from outside us – are not very effective. In fact, studies show they often decrease motivation, innovation and the pursuit of excellence. Far more powerful are intrinsic motivators, ones that emerge from inside us, such as the quest for mastery, the joy of autonomy, and the satisfaction of making progress in meaningful work.

Adding coaching techniques to your management style allows you to tap directly into those powerful intrinsic motivators so that the thinker can achieve great results. By creating a psychologically safe space for new thinking in the thinker, they grow new capability. Their confidence, engagement and excitement all go up. And, when the habits of coaching spread in a team or organisation, its confidence, engagement and excitement all go up, too. That is a team that can do anything.

What coaching isn't

Because the concept of a coaching style of management is unfamiliar, a blank spot in our thinking, I anticipate that readers might reach for familiar concepts to fill in the blank, such as counselling, mentoring or even training, but coaching is not these things, and the distinction is important.

Counselling is a talking therapy that tends to be about coming to terms with the past to heal current pain. That's not coaching. Coaching is a joint endeavour to discover new thinking about the future; it's supporting healthy, coping adults who want to achieve something new.

Nor is coaching mentoring. Mentoring is when you share your knowledge and experience with someone who is on a path you've already tread. That's not coaching. Coaching enables the thinker to forge their own path.

Coaching is not training, either. Training is about imparting a new skill or knowledge, while coaching assumes the thinker can already do what they need to do and supports them in figuring out how to overcome their barriers to get it done.

In short, coaching is not telling, advising, suggesting or leading the thinker's thinking. Coaching provides a process that supports the thinker in thinking more effectively for themselves.

Here's a situation in which you could use a coaching style. Someone is not performing to your expectation, it might be a member of staff, or it might be a subcontractor. Rather than telling them that they're not performing, which they probably know already, try asking them what might be holding them back. Then listen carefully. Then ask them what they might be able do about it. See what they come up with. This is basically the coaching conversation, and we'll explore it in more depth in Part 2.

'But, but ...'

When I talk to construction business leaders about this, they get it right away. Then almost as quickly there's a 'but ...'. 'But Dave,' they say, 'surely not every conversation can be a coaching conversation?' I understand this reservation. They worry that if they can't tell people what to do there will be anarchy. Projects will descend into chaos as inexperienced people get free rein to do whatever they want in the name of fulfilling themselves.

But they needn't worry. Of course you must give orders, especially when you spot unsafe or illegal things happening. And you can give advice, particularly when your people ask for it. (Withholding advice to force an unwanted coaching session defeats the purpose and is weird.) You can assert your authority and direct the team when you know from long experience that your way in this instance is best; coaching is not about reinventing the wheel. Nor is it being excessively nice, or debating everything under the sun, or tolerating incompetence and negligence. A construction project is not a democracy, and you're still the boss.

Instead, coaching should be thought of as a useful tool for challenging and supporting your people so they get better at thinking for themselves and so perform at consistently higher levels. If most of our conversations are giving orders, we're like the police, checking up on people and punishing non-compliance. If on the other hand we coach people by supporting them to figure things out for themselves, we're creating a workforce that is more engaged, more agile, more effective and hungrier for success. (Chapter 3 explores why coaching does this.)

So, while a coaching conversation is not appropriate in situations of danger and misconduct, I believe conversations in most other circumstances will be better and more effective if they are coaching conversations – better and more effective than ordering, telling, suggesting and leading. However, while the techniques of coaching are easy to start using, mastering them in the real world takes practice. Your goal should therefore be to steadily increase the proportion of coaching conversations you're having as you get better at having them. As a rough guide, beginner coach-managers might aim for 25% of their conversations to be coaching conversations; intermediate coach-managers might aim for 75%; and senior coach-managers 99.9%.

Your very first one could be when the thinker comes to you with a circumstance that is new to both of you, and that you can't try and solve for them by diving into their detail because you have your own job to do. That's a great opportunity to encourage new thinking, which can be added to the general pool of insight and experience.

Now let's turn to why construction companies need this.

CHAPTER 2

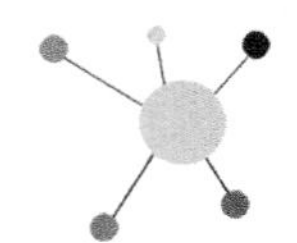

Why your company needs a coaching approach to management

Here, I'm going to spell out the reasons why construction in general, and your company in particular, needs this. In summary:

- Construction is foremost a people industry, but we act like it's not;
- Our default command-and-control management culture is ineffective and holds us back;
- Young construction professionals don't thrive in this culture, and it's preventing us from a) attracting and keeping talent, b) making our workforce more diverse, and c) improving our productivity – three tightly interlinked issues.

Let's explore this in a bit more detail.

Construction is foremost a people industry

We tend to think of construction as primarily a technical endeavour, but above all it is a people industry, and I say that as a chartered civil engineer. The technical disciplines give us designs, costs and a programme, but then total strangers must come together to turn those abstract data into a physical thing, in real time, under challenging conditions, over many months, with a grave deadline. It is a big, difficult result and yet, speaking from forty-five years' experience, we typically give zero thought as to how those people will work together. It's just left to individual styles, habits and chance.

We put our faith instead in the hard systems set up to control the outcome: contracts, the programme, project management protocols and software. They should keep everybody on track, but we know they don't always. Unexpected things happen, priorities diverge, commercial imperatives clash, opinions differ, emotions intervene. The world is the world, and we are people. Projects need hard systems but such systems don't guarantee success. Success relies on the chemistry that is always at play among people, which we ignore at our peril. When the chemistry is wrong, it breeds misunderstandings, conflict, defects and waste. A coaching management style fosters a positive, results-oriented chemistry. When a coaching management culture takes root in a team or organisation, that team or organisation is wired for success.

Our default command-and-control management culture is ineffective

What is our management culture now? In my experience the default management culture is command-and-control. We issue orders and use fear and blame to punish non-compliance. It's the style I absorbed when I entered the industry as a sixteen-year-old. Nowadays we're less shouty and sweary; we issue orders politely, but the basic command-and-control paradigm is intact. The problem with it is that it erodes trust and engagement, robs people of their agency and stifles initiative and creativity.

A coaching style of management does the opposite. It gives people ownership over their accountabilities and supports them in working out how best to fulfil them. This taps into powerful intrinsic motivators that, as we'll see, can be counted on to drive people to excel without you having to cajole and monitor them.

Where command-and-control assumes that I the manager know best about everything, coaching recognises that I don't, and calls on the talents and insights latent in the people around me. A team run by command-and-control is rigid and limited by what I as manager know and can conceive, whereas a coached team is smarter, nimbler and more capable because everybody's talent, knowledge and experience are pooled and harnessed. If you were a client, which sort of team would you want working for you?

Young professionals are not thriving in this culture

In 2020, we surveyed hundreds of construction professionals under the age of forty and found that some 57% of them would probably not recommend the industry as a career to friends and family. Only 27% were active promoters of the industry. In the wider world of business, that is a dangerously low level of engagement and job satisfaction.[1]

The reasons they cited were many and various: long hours, high pressure, poor culture and mentality, not enough diversity, a lack of opportunities to develop, and more. Analysing their comments, you would struggle to identify what in particular we could fix in order to increase engagement and job satisfaction across the board. But we do know one thing: research shows conclusively that managers play a huge role in employee engagement and job satisfaction. Analytics giant Gallup found that managers account for 70% of variance in employee engagement.[2] Plenty of studies show managers have a major impact on employees' job satisfaction, commitment to the organisation,

---

1 Our methodology is explained here: 'What our millennials really feel about the industry', by Dave Stitt. https://dsabuilding.co.uk/what-our-millennials-really-feel-about-the-industry/

2 Randall Beck and Jim Harter, 'Managers Account for 70% of Variance in Employee Engagement', Gallup, 21 April 2015. https://news.gallup.com/businessjournal/182792/managers-account-variance-employee-engagement.aspx

and what's called 'positive discretionary behaviours', or, in plain language, going the extra mile. As the management guru Marcus Buckingham observed, people join firms but leave their managers. Managers are the glue in engaged, high-performing teams; or they could be.

This matters for three important and interlinked reasons. One is our ongoing difficulty in recruiting and keeping talent; a second is our stubbornly un-diverse workforce; the third is our chronically poor productivity. These three issues are manifestations of construction's suboptimal management culture, and a coaching style of management addresses all of them. Let's take them one by one.

Our chronic skills crisis

For decades, we've wrung our hands over how difficult it is to recruit and keep talent, and we've blamed the industry's bad image. But what if this is a red herring, and the real problem is our off-putting, command-and-control management culture, which we tend to think is just normal? What if it's dysfunctional?

Senior people at the sharp end of construction – our managers – are not paid, incentivised or even trained in the people skills needed to nurture and develop the talent rising around them. They're paid, incentivised and trained to win and deliver projects in a risky, adversarial environment so, naturally, that is their focus. It means we don't give enough thought to the new people coming up behind us, those in their 20s and 30s who are trying to find their way in a complex, high-pressure industry.

In our research we spoke to dozens of young construction professionals, and it gave us a clear impression of what's at stake for them at the industry coal face. Put yourself in their shoes. Let's say you entered the industry without first being immersed in its culture, either through family connections or, as I was, in joining at a young, impressionable age. Imagine struggling trying to decipher the unwritten rules and work out what's expected of you. Your job excites you in principle, but you have to admit that the industry's culture is 'unique', for want of a better word. Your manager is under pressure, remote and seemingly indifferent to you and your development. At the same time, the pressure to deliver is immense. It's sink-or-swim.

Clearly, lots of young professionals hammer out their own accommodation with this unique culture, as I did. But what if that's just not you? Imagine not knowing if you're good or not, not knowing what getting better looks like, or how to do it. If you're struggling with that, you're not enjoying your career. You don't feel secure; you wonder if you're cut out for this. You watch your back and soldier on because you have to, for now. But would you recommend construction as a career? It doesn't seem likely.

Now consider that the most powerful influence on young people's views are not what adverts or talking heads say, but what other young people say. So what if, instead of a culture in which managers are remote, indifferent and demanding, they are instead available, interested and supportive of your development? That would lead to a lot of people loving their jobs. Now, just a quarter of young construction professionals would genuinely recommend the industry as a career choice to peers. Imagine if, in your company, that figure was 50%, or 70%, or 90%. That would be the most powerful recruiting tool you could conceive.

Our stubborn lack of diversity

To stay competitive, your company needs to attract and retain talent from sections of the population that currently avoid construction, including that half of it who are not male and other under-represented groups. I believe a coaching management culture will allow a company's workforce to become more diverse.

Why? Consider the culture of construction. The people who work in the industry are predominantly white and male. Left to its own devices, any culture breeds micro-cultures of exclusion. In these micro-cultures are implicit (unspoken) codes of behaviour and shared assumptions about what's acceptable and what isn't. This includes humour, what's considered fun, who is esteemed and why, conceptions of right and wrong, how conflict is handled, and more. These implicit codes govern who is welcome in the club and who isn't. It's just human behaviour; all humans seek out people who are like them, over and against those who are different.

Sadly, characteristics that have nothing to do with the work at hand, like gender, skin colour, accent and religious observance, can mean exclusion from the club. Sometimes, people with the 'wrong' characteristics can gain entry to the club if they understand the implicit codes and make a show of following them. This both reinforces the exclusionary micro-culture while furnishing the appearance of proof that it is not exclusionary. Those with the wrong characteristics who don't understand the implicit codes, or who are not minded to follow them, will find themselves shut out, deprived of warmth, support and a sense of belonging, even if there is no outright hostility.

The industry has come a long way in the forty-five years I've been in it. At the professional level, white, male, macho culture is far less prominent, but exclusionary micro-cultures still form under the surface in any part of any company, any time. An exclusionary micro-culture is a closed system, like a piece of proprietary software. To outsiders its rules are hidden and unintelligible. By contrast, a coaching management culture is open-source: the rules are explicit, intelligible and anyone can contribute according to them. In language terms, courtesy, respect and esteem are universal. The simple act of saying, and meaning it, 'What do you think?', is an invitation to join the club. It says,

'You're good, you're welcome, you're valued. Come in and help us.'

Can it really be that simple: a thing you say? Yes. How will our partners know we love them if we don't tell them? If we're serious, as professionals are supposed to be, we say what we mean, and if we mean it, we show it; our behaviour aligns with our speech. When it is a habit of your managers to say to their people, 'What do you think?', they are building an open, welcoming culture in which people can thrive, whatever their gender, race or religion. It is the antidote to exclusionary micro-cultures.

Our chronic productivity crisis

Productivity is the third interlinked issue; first because the cultural factors that make people unhappy in work also render teams prone to error and conflict, and second because a culture that repels swathes of the population is a culture that deprives itself of the very talent it needs to raise productivity.

After the disasters of the last decade – faulty Edinburgh schools, the Grenfell catastrophe, the collapse of Carillion – the response has been to tinker with systems: forms of contract, approaches to procurement and finance, project management protocols, regulations and quality assurance regimes. As I said above, this misses a crucial ingredient: culture at the company level, and the chemistry it breeds.

Systems can always be gamed and rules can be followed to the letter but not the spirit, especially in such a fragmented and adversarial industry like ours.

I spent twenty-five years at the coal face of delivering projects, and know the havoc bad chemistry causes. I've seen enough faulty slabs jackhammered out to know that mistakes happen routinely: big and small, often unreported. They erode margins, damage reputations and spark disputes. A command-and-control management style breeds bad chemistry. It sucks initiative, confidence and accountability out of a team. It puts too much onus on me, the command-and-control manager, to know everything, to issue the correct orders, and to enforce those orders. This is risky when a team is comprised of people from different companies whose commercial agendas are indifferent to the success of the project as a whole. You can threaten and assert, but people will go straight to the contract to see what precisely is the deliverable for which they can invoice, and offer not one iota more.

Good chemistry boosts productivity. We know what this looks like. People are pulling together to realise a clearly defined common goal. Everyone trusts each other to do the right thing in support of that goal. They are talking to each other frankly and honestly, so that information flows to where it's needed, when it's needed. Everyone is on high alert for anything that might jeopardise the result and they take timely and concerted effort to eliminate the risk. There is an *esprit de corps* of learning lessons and moving forward briskly; no one's that interested in blame and recrimination. The atmosphere is polite, open, welcoming and friendly. People feel valued.

Construction business leaders must ask themselves some tough questions. Are your younger staff being guided effectively into maturity as professionals, or are they being drawn into negative, exclusionary micro-cultures? Do your people know that quality is the top priority, along with everything else that must be top priority? Are your people empowered to spot quality issues, and the conditions that breed them, and speak up immediately? Are the relationships among your people good enough so that, working together, they can take action to head off quality issues when spotted? Are your people rewarded for taking this kind of collective initiative to ensure quality again and again? Each of these questions is a culture issue that must be addressed within a company.

Sometimes good chemistry happens in construction, such as when gifted managers are involved, but it's not the default setting. Thanks to the fragmented and adversarial nature of the industry, the default setting is more like the situation that arose among a construction team I worked with a few years ago, which I'll recount because it is illustrative. On a Friday afternoon the contractor's project manager got what he took to be a challenging email from the client's representative. The project manager took offence and spent the whole weekend compiling a defensive, six-page response, which he fired off Monday morning. This caught the client's representative off guard. It was startling and aggressive, and he took offence in turn. There ensued a war of angry correspondence that lasted several weeks. When we all got together I asked what was upsetting them so much, and it emerged that the client's representative had just wanted to understand certain aspects of the project but it had come out wrong in the email, leading to a huge, unproductive spillage of energy and goodwill. It could all have been avoided had the representative, or the project manager, just picked up the phone to talk things over.

You can't mandate good chemistry, you have to cultivate it. It starts with the behaviour of one capable manager who knows how to be normal, humane and polite. They set the example and expect others to follow it. And others will follow it, because good chemistry is contagious. It is natural, enjoyable and in tune with our psychological make-up. It has trouble taking root in the stony ground of construction, but it can. We can't change the fragmented, adversarial nature of the industry but we can choose not to be defined by it.

A coaching style of management is the easiest way for ungifted managers to start behaving in a way that fosters good chemistry. In essence, it is the simple decision to be normal, humane and polite. The coach-manager's stance toward the people who report to them is welcoming, not suspicious and demanding. All you have to say is: 'What do you think?', and then you have to listen. When we hear that – 'What do you think?' – something powerful happens. Even if the statement is delivered clumsily by a normally distant and awkward manager, we suddenly feel noticed, respected and valued. We feel pride, excitement and confidence. We look at the manager with new eyes. There are stirrings of trust, and we begin to articulate what we really think. The possibility of a positive relationship emerges, and we want to do our best.

This is how good chemistry is seeded in a team or organisation. You make yourself available as a respectful thinking partner to the people you manage, and they do the same with the people they manage, and so on. As this culture spreads, conversations change and the mood lifts; trust, excitement, enjoyment go up. Mistrust, stress, conflict and misunderstandings struggle to get a foothold.

Gallup has years worth of data showing the causal links between employee engagement and higher customer satisfaction, profitability, productivity and quality (fewer defects), lower staff turnover and fewer safety incidents. 'When a company raises employee engagement levels consistently across every business unit, everything gets better', they note.[3] And the most direct route to higher employee engagement, starting right now, is through a

---

[3] Ibid.

coaching style of management. Gallup chairman Jim Clifton got there before me in 2017, when he said organisations should phase out 'command-and-control managers' (his words) and bring in 'high-performance coaches' able to hold 'high-development conversations'.[4]

In this chapter I've made some claims that may run counter to readers' sense of how construction, and the world in general, ought to work. So, in the next chapter we're going to peek under the bonnet, as it were, and review the basic psychological underpinnings of the coaching style of management and why it gets better results, to show that it is not just right, but essential, for construction.

---

4 Jim Clifton, 'The World's Broken Workplace', Gallup, 13 June 2017. https://news.gallup.com/opinion/chairman/212045/world-broken-workplace.aspx

CHAPTER 3

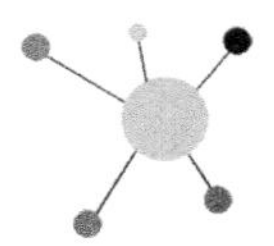

A peek under the bonnet: Why a coaching style works

We think of construction as a unique industry, and it is. From scratch, we build big, expensive, bespoke things that allow society to function. Over the decades, I've worked with countless talented, committed and loyal professionals who are intensely proud of what they do, and rightly so. But construction is also a business like other businesses, employing people who are just like everybody else, so our uniqueness goes only so far. And because we're a people industry, we can't afford to ignore insights into people management that have been shown to work in other industries. Companies seeking a competitive advantage in this industry right now should investigate what works and how it can be adapted. When I claim that managers using coaching techniques can create a workforce that is more engaged, agile, effective and hungrier for success, that claim is supported by studies in behavioural psychology. In this chapter, I'll explore two key insights from those studies that have emerged in the past decade, and which other sectors are putting to good use. They concern what really motivates us in the pursuit of excellence at work, and the primal importance of psychological safety in fostering a high-performance work culture. As I'll show, a coaching style of management is the easiest and most direct way for companies to begin making use of these insights.

I will also set out a philosophical proposition – a meta insight – that changed my life when it was first put to me in the days of leading culture-change programmes, and which has informed my work coaching executive teams in construction ever since. That proposition is this: relationships are the foundation of results. It's a simple truth, but one that has eluded construction. I'll show how the power of this proposition can be harnessed in our industry through a coaching style of management.

First, though, to the topic of motivation ...

What really motivates us?

For your team to do something uncommon you need team members who are uncommonly motivated. But how do you achieve that? It's an age-old problem, and solutions have tended toward the bizarre in recent years. I'm thinking about the recent flare-up of interest in 'happiness' as the magic bean of workplace motivation. Google and other trend-setting companies appointed 'chief happiness officers' to inject joy into work. 'Funsultants' are available to help firms spot and defeat outbreaks of gloom with games, unusual perks and team-building exercises. Academics are jumping on the bandwagon. A 2014 study led by researchers at the University of Warwick in England found that groups of workers shown a clip of a comedy film, or plied with chocolate, fruit and drinks, were more productive during a measured period than colleagues who received no such goodies. They concluded that these 'happiness treatments' improved productivity by as much as 12%,[1] although they stopped short of recommending that companies try this approach, because it's time-consuming and expensive.

To me this feels wrong, as if our emotions were fair pickings for employers to separate out and manipulate in order to get a desired response. Nor is it sustainable, especially if an employee's happiness, whatever we take that to mean, relies on external stimuli. What happens when people tire of chocolate and clowns? Surely, genuine motivation comes from within, so the real concern should not be how to keep people motivated *in spite of* their work, but how to arrange things so that they are motivated *by* their work.

---

[1] Andrew J. Oswald, Eugenio Proto, and Daniel Sgroi, 'Happiness and Productivity', *Journal of Labor Economics* 33, no. 4 (October 2015): 789-822. https://doi.org/10.1086/681096

My guide on this question is Daniel Pink, author of the splendid book, *Drive: The Surprising Truth About What Motivates Us* (Canongate, 2010). Pink challenged the theory of 'scientific management', developed in the late 1800s by American engineer Frederick Winslow Taylor, which held that workers must be managed through rewards (a pay cheque, a bonus) for doing what is required, and punished (fines, or being fired) for not doing what is required. Taylor's theory was called 'scientific' because it harnessed people's rational drive to put food on the table and to keep a roof over their head.[2] Daniel Pink argued that it doesn't work anymore. It was okay in the industrial age when most jobs were routine but now, when success in business requires initiative and innovation, people need something more than carrots and sticks to give it their all.

Money in particular is a questionable motivator, Pink observed. Clearly, people need adequate and fair recompense, but Pink cites numerous studies showing how money can actually stifle the most important things we want from employees – creativity, problem-solving and commitment. Artists produce inferior work when commissioned. Asked to solve puzzles, people get stupider if you introduce cash rewards. One classic study took three groups of children, all of whom liked drawing in their spare

---

[2] Taylor set out his theories in his 1911 book, *The Principles of Scientific Management*.

time. Group one was shown a fancy certificate and told they'd get one if they spent the session drawing. Group two were given their certificate as a surprise for drawing. And group three were invited merely to draw, without expecting a certificate or being surprised with one. Two weeks later, children from the second and third groups were still happily drawing, while children from the first group had drifted to other things. Researchers concluded that the expectation of a reward snuffed out their enjoyment of drawing. Overall, Pink said, extrinsic motivation – the promise of money or perks – promotes short-term thinking, undercuts the enjoyment of the activity, encourages shortcuts and cheating, and diminishes creativity and performance.

As a manager, you will be limited in terms of how much cash or perks you can dangle in front of your people. Pink's helpful insight is that it doesn't matter because there are better ways of engendering commitment, excitement and motivation. The trick is to allow for what he calls 'intrinsic' motivation to take hold, where the work itself inspires people. This happens when people get three crucial things from work: a sense of autonomy; a sense of mastery; and a sense of purpose. A command-and-control style of management leaves little room for these three things, whereas a coaching style of management explicitly fosters them.

Autonomy is when people have control over the fulfilment of their accountabilities. They decide how they do what they're meant to do. Command-and-control tightly restricts individual sovereignty, while coaching invites people to own their accountabilities and think independently about how to fulfil them.

Mastery is about giving people the opportunity to get better at something they care about, not for money or brownie points, but for the joy of it. It's when a person's unique suite of interests and capabilities can find expression in their work. People in construction care a great deal about their work. Coaching assists them in their pursuit of mastery, whereas command-and-control is more narrowly focused on rules and compliance.

Purpose gives people a sense that what they're doing has meaning beyond just drawing a salary. Pink argues that the quest for money alone has weakened as a motivator among two key demographic groups: Baby Boomers (born between 1946 and 1964), because they are approaching the end of their working lives and are beginning to feel pangs of the natural human hunger for meaning; and Millennials (people born from the mid-1980s) who seem to want meaning in large doses right from the start, and who are reluctant to step onto the career treadmill merely for the sake of it. Pink finds a growing number of organisations who deploy this appetite in various ways, either by linking profits to charitable works, or by allowing employees to divert some of their skills and time to causes that matter to them. This is good, but I would argue that purpose does not have to mean altruism. For many people, the pursuit of excellence, the fulfilment of one's potential, recognition, a happy client, and being a valued part of an important endeavour all constitute purpose. Because it values people for their talents, coaching makes a growing sense of purpose possible in the work they turn up daily to do.

Harnessing the power of intrinsic motivation can send a jolt of excitement coursing through an organisation, Pink says, and it also produces results nobody could have predicted. His crowning example is the story of Microsoft's *MSN Encarta*, and its rival, Wikipedia. In 1993 Microsoft launched its bid to create the world's first digital encyclopaedia. Expert writers and editors were paid to craft articles on everything under the sun. Microsoft's finest managers were tasked with launching it as a CD-ROM and later as a website, with its premium version available for a fee. Business development people built up revenue streams in online subscriptions, CD-ROM sales and online advertising. It spent millions buying up Funk & Wagnalls and Collier's encyclopaedias. But despite throwing everything it had at the project, Microsoft finally pulled the plug on 31st December 2009, admitting that people just didn't look up information that way anymore. Compare that to Wikipedia. Launched in 2001 by a handful of enthusiasts, Wikipedia by 2009 had become the seventh most visited website in the world; its millions of articles in more than 240 languages contributed and edited by volunteers, for the hell of it, because it made them happy. The fact that it is powered for free by amateurs – a word derived from the French word for love – remains a testament to the potency of intrinsic motivation.

Pink describes numerous experimental approaches companies have taken in an attempt to foster intrinsic motivation but, for many organisations, they are complicated and disruptive to roll out as HR policy. Top-down novel approaches usually are. The beauty of a coaching management style is that any of your people can just start doing it, today.

Psychological safety

As powerful as intrinsic motivation is, it can't be harnessed adequately without another crucial ingredient in the culture of an organisation: psychological safety. A psychologically safe work culture is one where people can speak freely without fear of embarrassment or punishment. It's one that encourages open and frank dialogue, the point being to seek truth and get good ideas. Such a culture knits people activated by intrinsic motivation together to achieve uncommon results. It can be created or killed by managers at all levels in your organisation.

Here, my guide is Amy C. Edmondson, Novartis Professor of Leadership and Management at Harvard Business School, whose acclaimed book, *The Fearless*

Organisation (Wiley, 2019), introduced the concept to the business world and has been translated into eleven languages. Edmondson's starting point is that in the knowledge economy, companies need innovation, creativity and 'spark' to flourish, which entails attracting and keeping high-quality talent, and hitching that talent to a goal.

Perhaps we don't think of construction as a 'knowledge industry' but, in my view, it most definitely is. The knowledge of designers, planners, estimators, specifiers, project managers, specialists, constructors and more must be pooled, organised and transformed into a physical thing, on time and on budget. To do that requires innovation, creativity and spark every hour of the day. Problems – physical, commercial, political – come at us continually from every direction and threaten to blow a project off course, and those problems need effective, collective responses. I often feel that the amount of innovation, creativity and spark it takes to execute projects, even ones that don't make headlines, is remarkable and largely uncelebrated. But we can't be complacent and assume we've got it covered, because we haven't.

Baby Boomers like me assumed it was fine to use fear to motivate people but, as Edmondson points out, this is counterproductive. Neuroscience tells us that fear inhibits learning and impairs memory, analytical thinking and problem-solving. If your people need to solve a problem, you need them to be thinking clearly, laterally and creatively about the best way forward, and to be able to share their thoughts. Your people will almost certainly see things that you don't, and you all need to hear it. When people feel it's safe to contribute their insights, the knowledge in the room shoots up. On the other hand, when organisations foster a culture of deferential silence, one where bad news and divergent views are unwelcome, and where elephants in the room go unmentioned, they are heading for trouble. Such a culture of frightened deference was claimed to be a contributing factor in the demise of Carillion.[3]

Psychologically unsafe work cultures are quite common in construction and, unfortunately, it often emanates from the top. I witnessed it in the board of directors of a construction firm I coached. The company was having difficulties, but the board met as a group only once every three months, and all they discussed on those occasions was profit and loss and troublesome projects. A few months into the programme one of them spoke up, saying: 'We never give each other feedback or talk about how we're doing as a team.' It was an honest remark, intended constructively, but it went down like a lead balloon. Everyone shifted uncomfortably in their seats. I suggested a basic feedback-sharing method, and asked if they'd like to try it. They

---

[3] Rob Davies, 'Carillion was in trouble by mid-2016, says whistleblower', *The Guardian*, 22 February 2018: https://www.theguardian.com/business/2018/feb/21/carillion-was-in-trouble-by-mid-2016-says-whistleblower

looked nervous and reluctant. There was too much baggage. Clearly, they worried that honest feedback would descend into blame and recrimination. There was no psychological safety. But, admirably, they gave it a go and, starting with small steps, they soon had a working feedback mechanism that created a safe environment for them to increase their candour. Up went their confidence, as did their sense of what they could do collectively. They began encouraging the practice throughout the organisation, and its results improved accordingly.

Beyond the boardroom, managers have the power to create micro-climates of psychological safety. It takes a deliberate effort, however. There are things you have to do; it won't happen on its own. In my experience, unless there is a deliberate effort, teams will drift naturally into a deferential silence that suppresses information and insight, until there's a crisis. It's a function of organisational entropy as people subside into routine in search of a quiet life.

You have to get people together. You have to frame the discussion and create a shared understanding of the situation, setting out what's at stake and what failure and success look like. Then you have to invite feedback. Here, there are rules. Feedback must be constructive, not personal criticism. The conversation takes the form of suggestions and observations, not assertions and demands, because it's a dialogue requiring everyone's contribution, not a debate to be won or lost. At the end, everyone understands that the final decision rests with you; there will not be a vote. Finally, you as manager need to set the example of conducive behaviour. Acknowledge you don't know everything; ask questions and listen carefully; thank people and praise them for their accomplishments and contributions. With encouragement from the boardroom, psychologically safe micro-climates can proliferate and spread until it is the dominant culture of an organisation.

I probably don't need to spell this out, but a coaching style of management constitutes the first step in fostering a psychologically safe work culture. The very act of saying to the people who report to you, 'What do you think?', creates the space for them to open up. What you do next will be covered in Part 2.

We turn now to the meta insight that encapsulates why construction business leaders should pay attention to intrinsic motivation, psychological safety and other positive effects of a coaching style of management: relationships are the foundation of results.

Relationships are the foundation of results

In construction, we tend to think the foundation of results is action. When results are not materialising, we think we need bigger, harder, faster action. We throw more people at the job, pound the table at subcontractors, cancel leave and work all hours of the day. But what if we've got that wrong?

One of the first coaching concepts I learned when I moved into the field of corporate culture change some twenty-five years ago changed my life and became the lodestar of my work. Put forward by the American thinker Werner Erhard, it states simply that the real foundation of results is not action, but relationships. Let's explore this idea.

On the face of it, results do stem from actions. But there is a lot more going on under the surface here. They cannot be just any old actions; they need to be the right ones. The ability to select the right actions to solve a problem depends on the range of actions available to you, and the more choice you have, the better. The range of actions available to you depends on the opportunities that are available. Opportunities to take action consist of things that manifest in the real world, and what turns those things into opportunities for action are possibilities.

Possibilities are not things that manifest in the real world; instead, they are ideas and thoughts that emerge from people's imaginations, based on their experience, expertise and knowledge. Possibilities are usually expressed as 'What if?' questions that spark the hunt for opportunities. Because possibilities emerge from people's imaginations, you need good relationships with people in order to discover fruitful possibilities. So, the quantity and quality of your relationships determine the quantity and quality of the possibilities that emerge. It's why we say we need to 'get our heads together' or 'pool our thinking' to solve a problem.

This dynamic is mapped in Figure 1, the Results Pyramid.[4]

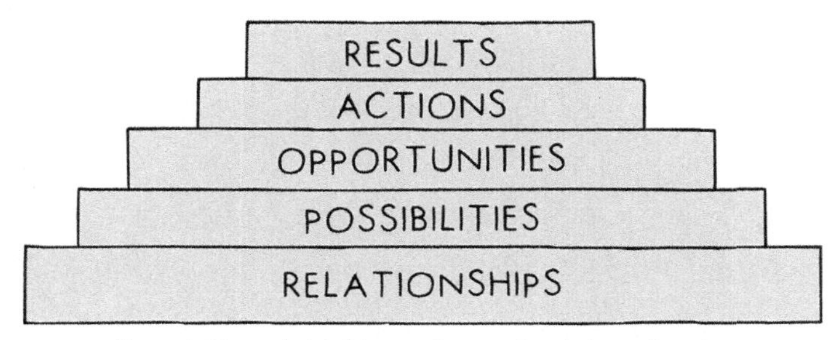

Figure 1. How relationships are the true foundations of results.
(Credit: Landmark Worlwide LLC and Werner Erhard, reproduced with permission)

Here's a scenario showing how it works. Let's say I live near a dangerous junction, where there are often collisions. I decide to ask my local town councillor about getting a roundabout built to regulate traffic better. The councillor isn't keen because it'll cost money, but says she'll raise the issue. Nothing happens. Fuming, I make a sign, saying 'Honk if you want a roundabout here!' and wave it by the junction at rush hour. All I get is hostile looks.

Tired of my complaining, my wife suggests I call a local meeting. I've never done anything like that before but, lacking any other plan, I do. I put up notices inviting people to the community centre to discuss the issue. On the night, only a handful of people show up, which is disappointing. What's more, I have trouble keeping the discussion on topic, because the participants, who are mostly elderly, seem keener to gossip and reminisce.

Then, just as I'm about to give up, a woman called Mabel

claps her hands. 'Right folks,' she says, 'young Dave here is raring to go on this roundabout business, so let's put our heads together. I was thinking we could set up a Facebook page. My daughter's always campaigning for this and that on Facebook.' Then a man called Nigel says he used to work for the council and knows where to find the data on road accidents. If it showed our junction to be a trouble spot, that would make interesting reading on the Facebook page. Then June pipes up, saying she could raise money for the campaign through a crowdfunding site. Melissa knows people at the local TV station, and could maybe organise some coverage. Victoria says she can make videos, and that we could do a video explaining why we need a stop sign to put on the Facebook page. I go home exhilarated; none of that would ever have occurred to me. Within a couple of months, hundreds of people are calling for a roundabout and the councillor has to act.

We can make some observations about this scenario, keeping the Results Pyramid in mind. First, I got nowhere with the councillor because my relationship with her was weak. I am only one of many constituents; she owes no special obligation to me, and what I asked of her was boring and irksome. The action I took, waving a sign, was drastic but fruitless. But then, when I activated my local web of human relationships, interesting and unforeseen possibilities emerged. These possibilities could then be actuated by the opportunities available: social media, data, skills, money, contacts. The actions that followed could well have achieved the desired result. Note, too, that the apparently idle chit-chat that frustrated me – Action Man – at the start of the meeting was actually the participants doing important relationship-building work, and wise Mabel knew when enough was enough.

The lesson contained in this little scenario will be familiar to everyone: big things can happen when people come together. A broader relationship base leads to more potent possibilities, which in turn leads to more diverse opportunities and more effective actions. In theory, this is so obvious it's a cliché, but in reality it is widely ignored in organisational life, especially in construction, where we often behave as if it doesn't apply. So, next time you are struggling to achieve the required results, instead of diving into bigger, harder faster actions, step back and ask: do we have the relationships we need, and are those relationships big enough to deliver the results we want? Most often, they won't be, and that's where you need to focus your attention.

However, you have to start in your own zone. The most important relationships are the ones between you and your team, the ones among your team members, and outward, between your team members and the people outside your zone they are interacting with. Because it recognises the value of the other person, a coaching style of management facilitates big relationships. A 'big' relationship is one based on trust, communication and a mutual desire to help. When a coaching management culture is seeded in a business unit, the unit seeks big relationships beyond itself, which spreads the culture.

This part of the book has been about the 'what' and the 'why' of a coaching approach to management. I've tried to set out how a coaching style of management activates the talent and commitment lying latent in your people by tapping into what really motivates them and fostering an atmosphere of psychological safety, which teams need to excel. I've outlined why construction companies need this in order to tackle the chronic, and linked, problems of talent scarcity, a lack of diversity and poor productivity. Now it's time to get down to brass tacks: how do you do it?

---

[4] Some of the materials in this chapter, specifically the 'Results Pyramid', are the property of Landmark Worlwide LLC and Werner Erhard, and are used with permission.

PART TWO

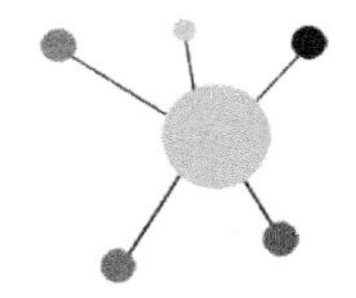

The How

CHAPTER 4

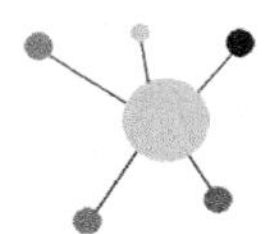

Life is a conversation

Twenty-five years ago, my first coach said to me, 'Dave, life is a conversation.' I said, 'What do you mean?' 'Think about it,' he said, and I have been ever since.

Success in getting out-of-the-ordinary things done depends on the conversations you're having. In fact, I have a formula to express this. It goes: *Your capacity for success equals the conversations you're having, minus the conversations you're not having, multiplied by the quality of the conversations you're having.*

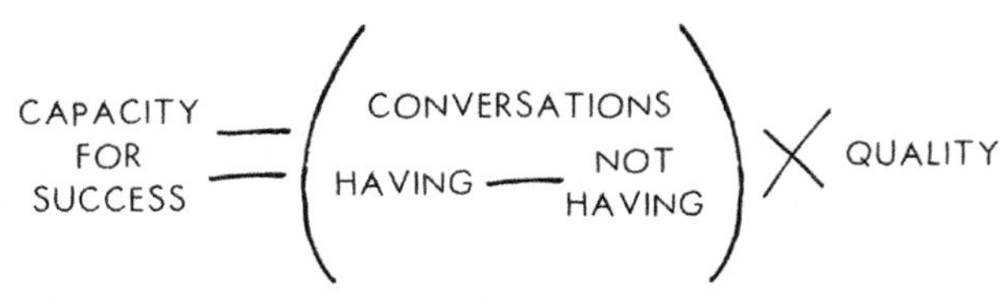

Figure 2. Conversations Success Formula. (Credit: Dave Stitt)]

Let's unpack this.

To get tricky things done, you need information and

help. The fastest way to get information is to ask people who know, and the fastest way to get help is to ask people who can help. That means you need to converse with people, and the more people the better.

What's a high-quality conversation? It's one where the two of you gain a deeper appreciation of each other's worlds and objectives, which leads to a negotiation over how you can help each other, followed by a mutual commitment to do so. Good conversations are multipliers for success. Perhaps you can think of a time when you met just the right person who knew essential things you did not about something you were trying to do, and they were willing to help. I certainly can. Such conversations lead to giant and unexpected leaps forward. Remember that the foundation of results is relationships, and the currency of relationships is conversation.

To coach is to start conversations of a particular type. A coaching conversation has a job: to enable more effective thinking on the thinker's part about how they can move forward. As a manager, you need to be having these sorts of conversations with your team. But coaching techniques, like asking questions, listening, noticing and reflecting what you notice back to the thinker, are very useful in fostering good conversations in general, because they help to establish trust and rapport. A team that is in the habit of fostering good conversations with itself is equipped to foster good conversations outside itself.

And what about the conversations you're not having? Maybe because somebody upset you in the past and you don't like them, or because you don't actually know who can help? This is hurting your chances of success. If it's because of a grudge, have a think about how you can re-establish some constructive contact. You don't have to like a person, but you can still learn what they know, gain a deeper appreciation of their world and objectives, and negotiate your way to mutual assistance. Results are more important than grudges.

If you don't know who to ask, find out. Start initiating good conversations to find out who else you need to have good conversations with.

What are low-quality conversations? A low-quality conversation is one that fails to enhance mutual understanding and cooperation, or worse, that sows resentment and anger, such as in the case of the completely unnecessary standoff between the contractor's camp and the client's camp I described in Chapter 2.

A note on this: you cannot have high-quality conversations by email or text. Emails and texts can be ignored or misinterpreted, as happened above. With email, we think we're communicating, but really we're just transmitting words. Albert Mehrabian, a pioneer on the understanding of communications since the 1960s, found that in the communication of feelings and attitudes – which is what relationships are made of – only 7% of the spoken message is received through the words themselves; 38% of the message comes through the tone of voice; and 55% of it comes through body language, mostly from eye contact.

Dealing in words only, text and email are weak, low-bandwidth media. People need to see and hear the words you speak coming out, and you need to see and hear your words going in. Face to face, they can see 'where you're coming from', that is, they can sense your attitudes and feelings. They can understand your perspective and empathise. They can also ask questions to clarify what's required of them, and ask for assistance in return – in other words, negotiate. Face to face, assurances can be given, bargains made, and confidence instilled all in minutes with the help of looks, gestures, demeanour and tone of voice. Hammering it out by email would take hours, days even, and still leave lots of room to wriggle or for grave misunderstandings. People can tell themselves that, having crafted and sent a long email, they have 'got their point across', that they have 'set things straight' and that if the recipient doesn't get it then it is their problem and there is nothing more to be done. This is not the case at all and is often why endeavours fail. Email is fine for simple transactions and informing people of things, but big results require big relationships, and big relationships require big conversations.

So remember: *Your capacity for success equals the conversations you're having, minus the conversations you're not having, multiplied by the quality of the conversations you're having.*

Here is something to try. Think of a work challenge you face. Now think of a person in your organisation who might be able to help you deal with that challenge. It should be someone you don't interact with a lot, and who wouldn't expect an approach from you. How might you strike up a high-quality conversation with that person, with a view to enlisting their help?

CHAPTER 5

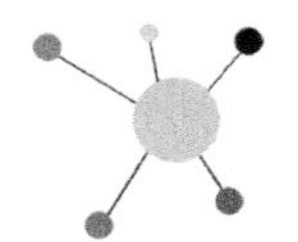

The Coaching Process: More golf than tennis

When you apply coaching techniques in your management style, you're initiating a partnership between you and the person you're coaching. It's a joint endeavour to help them discover new thinking. Why new thinking? Because if you want to get somewhere different, you have to do new things. Doing more of the same results in more of the same. Since thought precedes action, your old thinking probably won't get you where you want to be, so you have to engage in new thinking. New thinking leads to new insights, new actions and new results. When I talk about this with clients they sometimes worry that I expect them to dream up amazing new insights right there on the spot. I don't. New thinking doesn't have to be Einstein-level analysis, just thinking they haven't thought before in relation to what they're thinking about.

As a coach, I can tell the difference between old and new

thinking. When you say, 'What do you think?', what often comes out first is old thinking. Old thinking is well practised. The person will have told their story many times, so they have it down pat. In their old thinking, they are expert; it comes out all smooth and joined up, like a sales pitch.

You can disrupt the routine of old thinking with a question. The question should be neutral, signalling your curiosity about their thinking and encouraging them to develop it, as opposed to directly challenging their thinking by pointing out what's wrong with it. 'What about X?', you can say. The coaching conversation is an exploration, not a debate.

This leads to new thinking, and new thinking looks different. People hesitate, stumble and search the ceiling. They correct themselves, change their minds and lapse into silence. This is what new thinking looks like and, when you see it, don't interrupt! They're the thinker and they're doing their work. Resist the temptation to fill the silence with helpful suggestions and remarks.

As a manager using a coaching style, you're responsible for the coaching process and the thinker is responsible for their work and their future. Coaching happens through conversations, and the coaching conversation has a beginning, a middle and an end. We'll cover each of those in detail in subsequent chapters, but here's an overview. The beginning of the coaching conversation is working out what the thinking work will be today, here, in this conversation. The middle is to do the thinking work, and the end is to check we've done the work, finish it smoothly, and identify the thinker's new insights and actions. The results of this process often show up after the coaching conversation, when the thinker responds differently, more effectively, in work and life.

Here's an analogy. Coaching is more like playing golf than tennis. In golf, you and I progress together through the course from tee to green. If you hit the ball into the long grass, then, together, we work out what to do next to move forward. In tennis, it's you and your opponent whacking the ball back and forth, trying to score points. Coaching is a partnership between the coach and the thinker to move forward, and the coach stands slightly behind the thinker because the thinker is leading the way.[1]

Say a person who reports to you is struggling with an issue. Let's call her Jane. Jane has identified a clash in the design and the structural engineers are not responding to her Request for Information (RFI). Days have become weeks, she's getting worried, and isn't sure what to do. You're not either, because you're not familiar with the details, and you have your own things to worry about. You've asked for her thoughts, and she has rehearsed her old thinking on the issue, and has moved on to new thinking by talking through

---

[1] For the golf analogy, and much else, I am grateful to Claire Pedrick and her excellent book, *Simplifying Coaching*, Open University Press, 2020.

her options. 'What else?', you ask. She talks more, thinking aloud, and then decides on the next step. You let her take that step. She is now moving forward. This is how coaching works.

This response from you as manager may run counter to habit. It might be your habit is to try and solve her problem for her by diving into her detail and prescribing her next step. That's not coaching, and is not the best use of your time. It's her problem, and she should solve it. That is getting results through people. Before we can modify our habitual responses, however, we need to be aware of what they are. So try this. Notice your next three working conversations with members of your team. Are you moving together from tee to green, or are you playing tennis? Are you encouraging their new thinking, or trying to correct their old thinking? Notice these conversations and reflect on how you can modify your approach so the two of you can start moving forward together. Identify one thing you can start doing, and two things you could stop doing, so that your conversations become more effective.

Remember, we're learning a coaching style of management here, not turning you into professional coaches. Try it and relax – there is no perfect. See what works, and do more of that. Reflect on what didn't work, yet, and why. Have a go.

CHAPTER 6

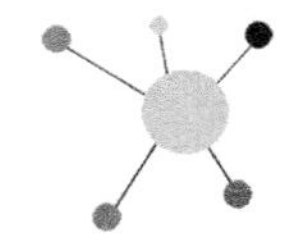

Starting the coaching conversation

Jane made you aware of the problem with her RFI, and it's a serious problem, one that could blow the project off course if it isn't handled carefully. You resisted the urge to take the problem over by diving into her detail and prescribing a solution because it's her accountability to fulfil and she is smart and resourceful, and you have your own accountabilities. So, you initiated a coaching conversation by inviting her to share her thinking about her problem, the aim being to enable her to think better and more confidently about what to do next.

Let's look more closely now at what happens at the start of the coaching conversation, because it needs to be designed in a way that can accommodate different sorts and lengths of encounters. Coaching conversations can take place anywhere and anytime, whether passing in the corridor, in a ten-minute telephone call, or in a scheduled meeting.

We use a concept called 'rightsizing' to start the conversation. Rightsizing is adjusting the scope of the conversation to fit the time we've got right now. In too many conversations, people turn up and pitch a scope that is galactic, as if the goal was to solve world hunger in twenty minutes. Invariably, twenty minutes later, world hunger is not solved and everyone leaves frustrated. We need the discipline to design the conversation so that it fits into the slot we've got; so, together, we'll work out what we're going to do here, right now, how we're going to do it, and how we'll know we've done it.

To rightsize, you can use a tool called STARS.

In STARS, 'S' is the Subject. What do we need to think about today? What question does Jane feel is most important right now? It might be, 'How can I increase pressure for a response to my RFI without getting people's backs up?'

'T' is Time. How long have we got for this conversation? Is it 10 minutes, an hour, two hours?

'A' is for Achieve. What specifically does Jane want to achieve in the time we have, and how will we know we've achieved it? It might be, 'I want to identify three, low-risk things I can do in the next twenty-four hours to raise the issue with the right people'.

'R' is Roles. How are we going to work together? What's your role, what's the thinker's role?

'S' is Start. Where does the thinker want to start? They're leading the way. It's their work and you as coach are accompanying them.

What you can do now is start practising rightsizing with STARS in the conversations you're having, whether they be coaching conversations or not. Meetings are very often poorly scoped, with people who like the sound of their own voice setting out to boil the ocean, so your new discipline will be appreciated by your busy colleagues. For the next few conversations, try rightsizing. Work out what you'd like to achieve in the time available. Come up with specific outcomes. Then compare that with what you actually achieve. Did you overshoot? Did you undershoot? What did you learn about yourself?

Remember, you're learning a coaching style here, not how to be a professional coach, so relax and have a go. If you don't get something exactly right, nothing bad will happen. See what works and what doesn't, and reflect on why.

CHAPTER 7

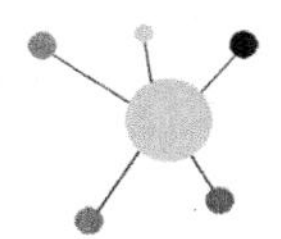

The middle of the coaching conversation

Once the coaching conversation gets going, your job is to maintain the space in which the thinker can think. The tools that will help you do this are 1) asking questions, 2) listening, 3) feedback and 4) goal-setting.

Asking questions is important because, when you tell someone something, or give them advice, their brain switches off. They stop thinking, except to find reasons why you're mistaken or what you're saying doesn't apply to them. When you ask questions, they have to start thinking. The questions shouldn't be barbed, or pre-loaded with your views. That'll provoke a defensive reaction and shut down their thinking. Make the questions neutral, to invite better thinking.

The key to asking better questions is to listen to your colleague carefully, actively. This will give you material to work with. Active listening is not mere passive hearing, waiting for the person to stop talking so you can start. Search for 'active listening' and you will find plenty of tips, but my favourite three are:

1. Prove you are listening by repeating back to the thinker what they are saying, with, for instance, 'So what you are saying is …' and 'If I'm hearing you correctly …'. Do it a lot, to an exaggerated degree. Less is not more in this instance. It will assure the thinker they're being heard and understood. This will increase their confidence to ask themselves, 'What do I really think?' It also gives you time to think and to formulate more effective questions.
2. Make no hard and fixed judgements on their position.
3. Don't react to trigger words and phrases that intentionally or not cause you offence or irritation. Focus on what they are saying, not on the feelings welling up inside you. Do notice, though; there will be a time to bring it up.

Listen especially for the thinker's here-and-now, the circumstances that are live, current and undigested. This is distinct from the there-and-then, the context and backstory, which the thinker is more confident in talking about because it's over, processed, packed away in its box. Ask about the here-and-now and what it means for the future, which is the focus of coaching, not reviewing the past.

Feedback, an extension of active listening, entails you noticing what you notice about the thinker, and reflecting that back to them without your interpretation, opinion, or diagnosis. Just simply notice. 'You sure?' you might say, or, 'That was a big sigh?' This encourages the thinker to open up more about what they're thinking and feeling, and why.

Goal-setting is the final piece of the puzzle. The thinker might come away from the coaching conversation with a plan for what to do next: what they need to find out, who they need to talk to, what decisions need to be made, by when, and anything else that moves them forward. The goals here are not the big, final project goals, but the countless, small, intermediate outcomes that move a project to completion.

In the last chapter we saw how rightsizing is necessary at the start of the coaching conversation to scope the conversation so it can achieve useful outcomes in the time available. Rightsizing can be used in the middle of the conversation as well, if the thinker goes off on a tangent. If they have wandered down a path that is different from the one you agreed to at the beginning, mention this. If they respond with, 'Actually, this is more important, this is what I really need to work on', that's fine. They're thinking, and they're leading, so together you rightsize the new subject for the remaining time. You can say, 'We have twenty minutes left. What do we need to think about for this to be useful to you?'

CHAPTER 8

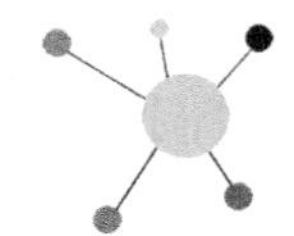

Ending the coaching conversation

The coaching conversation is like a flight. It has a take-off, a cruise at forty thousand feet, and a landing. The take-off is when you rightsize and agree the work that can be done in the time available. The middle is doing the work, when you're in the air at forty thousand feet. And the end is the landing. This chapter is about having a smooth landing.

Pilots start planning for landing long before they tell the cabin crew to get ready. It's the same with coaching. Suddenly announcing we've run out of time is a crash landing, and it's jarring and unpleasant for all. So, start planning for the end about halfway through the conversation.

There is a tool for this. It's called ACT. 'A' stands for Achieve and the actions needed to achieve the desired result. So, in preparation for landing, be asking, 'Where are we with what you wanted to achieve today?', and also,

'What's the first step to achieving that outside this conversation?'That points toward the necessary actions. Ask this a few times, as it will help the thinker develop a clearer idea of what specific actions to take.

'C' stands for Commitment. You'll want the thinker to feel committed to the actions they've identified, So ask, 'On a scale of nought to ten, how committed are you to moving forward on your action or insight?' If the number is above five, that signals commitment to at least a moderate degree. If the number is low, ask, 'Okay, what are you committed to?', and the thinker will respond. It might just be, 'Well, I need to think about this.' And thinking about something is okay; it's a fine outcome from a coaching conversation. It's unrealistic to expect the thinker to do all the necessary thinking right there in the conversation with you. They are telling you it's time to stop the coaching conversation so they can think.

'T' is Time. You ask by when they will have done the thing they've committed to doing. This is just about as bossy as a coaching style of management gets, but the purpose isn't to get a deadline on the table so you can hold it against them, but to shore up the thinker's own commitment to getting the thing done.

ACT is a good way to begin preparing for a smooth landing from about the middle of the coaching conversation because it ties up loose ends as you go and brings increasing focus to what the thinker will do after. I often end by bringing it to a sharper point by asking, 'What's your big takeaway today?' That helps it stick in their minds.

Time presents an interesting conundrum for the coach. You have to be disciplined about timekeeping because you're both busy and the coach must respect the thinker's boundaries, of which time is one. That is you modelling coaching behaviour. On the other hand, the coach mustn't ever rush the thinker. The veteran coach Claire Pedrick suggests that coaches be 'unconditionally positive' about time.[1] Instead of treating time as a precious commodity that is slipping through our fingers, ever at risk of being wasted – 'We've only got five minutes left!' – treat it as a friend you can count on to give the help that's needed – 'We've got a good five minutes left, what would you find it useful to think about?'

---

1 Claire Pedrick is the author of *Simplifying Coaching*. On time, see her LinkedIn blog, 'Never Enough Time', 27 May 2016. https://www.linkedin.com/pulse/never-enough-time-claire-pedrick-mcc/?trk=mp-reader-card

CHAPTER 9

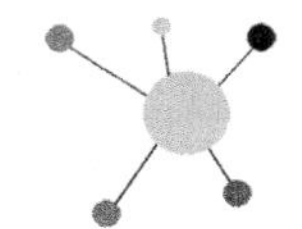

When to coach

Now that we've had a look at the mechanics of the coaching conversation, it's natural to ask, 'When should I as manager initiate a coaching conversation?' A related question is: should I be doing this all the time with everybody I manage?

The first question is a good one for new coach-managers who are starting to shift from command-and-control to a coaching style. Circumstances will make it apparent if you've already decided that you want to make yourself more available to the people who report to you. Think of Jane's trouble with her RFI. She told you about it because it's troubling her and she knows you need to know. That constitutes an opening: Jane needs some support. You can't solve her problem by diving into her detail and prescribing a way forward because that would take hours and you might get it wrong and you have enough on your plate as it is.

Jane wouldn't welcome that, anyway – not if she wants to progress in capability and experience. So, she needs support, but also challenge. The challenge is that the problem stays with her and she must solve it, but you're offering to accompany her in her thinking for a bit, even for thirty minutes, which will boost her morale and help her clarify her thoughts so she can take action, secure in the knowledge that you think she can do it and that her thinking is sound. When you say, 'What are you thinking about this?', she will take you up on the offer, and then you're away. It can and should be that natural.

Skilful managers take care to mix support with challenge. In their book, *Challenging Coaching*, John Blakey and Ian Day provide an extremely useful insight into this mix with their Support-Challenge Matrix.

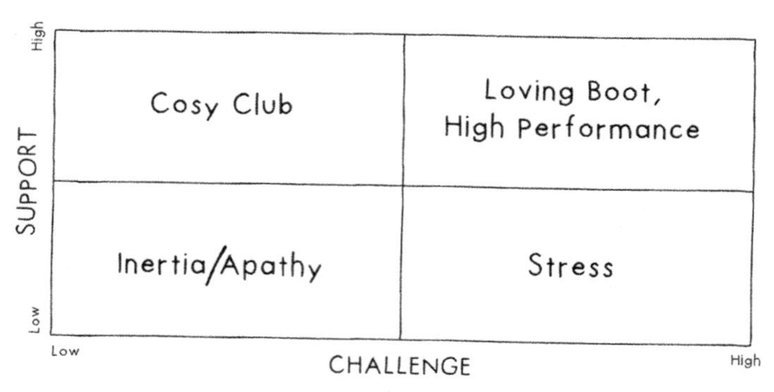

Figure 3. The Support-Challenge Matrix, from *Challenging Coaching*, by John Blakey and Ian Day. Reproduced with authors' permission.

When indifferent managers provide little support and little challenge, their people are in the zone of inertia, apathy, isolation and boredom. The manager doesn't care much, and neither will they. Work is meaningless. When managers are all challenge and no support – 'You did it wrong!', 'If you can't do this I'll find someone who can!' – because they are sadistic or are not coping themselves, their people experience mostly stress, which is debilitating. This is the zone of low morale, blame, backbiting, risk aversion and uneven performance. Placed in this zone for too long, people burn out or jump ship. When managers are all support and no challenge, they are coddling their people. This is the zone of complacency ('Cosy Club' is the term Blakey and Day coined), characterised by low standards, low achievement, a sense of entitlement, and stasis. Good managers – coach-managers – wade in with lots of both support and challenge. The bigger the result required, the more support and challenge you'll need. Blakey and Day call this the 'Loving Boot' quadrant. It's the zone of excitement, growth, purpose, high performance and consistently good results. Challenge originates not from your sniping and nastiness, but from the big results the team has signed up to deliver, of which you are custodian, and which translate into clear, intelligible, shared expectations that you articulate and uphold. This is you as leader. Coaching is the most efficient and effective way to offer the right mix of support and challenge.

Should you be doing this all the time with everybody you manage? Yes, mostly. When you get used to initiating coaching conversations just by asking 'What do you think?', you'll find it can be used in almost any situation bar a dangerous or illegal one, and to good effect.

Let's look at this scenario. You're the project manager on a very restricted site with not much storage area, nor room for site cabins. When the cabins were set up, it was known they'd have to be moved because they're on the line of a new drainage run to be installed. That time is fast approaching and, right now, the guy in charge of the drainage subcontractor, we'll call him Sam, is coming toward you on site with something clearly on his mind.

'Hi, yeah, listen,' Sam says, barging straight in. 'When are you going to shift those cabins? We've been waiting for ages.'

The question is unwelcome because you're not exactly sure when you're going to move the cabins yet.

Now, if you were me back when I was a command-and-control supremo, you might have responded aggressively, like this:

'I've told you before, Sam, we'll move them when we're ready, and anyway you've got plenty to be getting on with. And while you're here, you still haven't sorted out that defective concrete surround to MH6. So until that's done and backfilled we can't finish off that hardstanding area, so don't talk to me about us holding you up, that area is far more important to us than the last tail under our cabins.'

And he walks off, angry, thinking: 'What a useless project

manager! Can't he see we're trying to get this job built? And the defective concrete came from him!'

But you're not me as I was. You're a pretty dab hand at the coaching conversation now, and this is how it plays out.

'Hi, yeah, listen,' Sam says, barging straight in. 'When are you going to shift those cabins? We've been waiting for ages.'

And you say: 'Oh hey Sam, you got time to think it through together?'

'Oh, ah, well,' Sam says, considering. 'I'm just off to collect the wages, but yeah, let's give it ten minutes now.'

'Okay, great. What's on your mind?'

'Well, gang one is just about worked up and I'm looking for their next drop. I know they have that manhole to sort out which will take a few days. But after that I might have to off-hire the 360 excavator if the drain run under your cabin is not available for us to go at. We can get it back at a later date, though transport on the low loader costs us a packet. Although, I could use it to double up on gang two's work. The JCB they're using is just about on its limit at that depth, so the 360 could excavate while the JCB followed up with backfilling.'

(Sam is doing new thinking!)

'So,' you say, 'timing?'

'Well,' Sam says, looking over at the cabins (thinking), 'I reckon we need to be starting the drain run under your cabins a week on Monday. I'll let you know as soon as we've sorted that manhole and got it backfilled so you can relocate your cabins there, that's where you are putting them, isn't it?'

'Yes, brilliant, thanks Sam. What else?'

'No, that's fine,' Sam says, 'Thanks for your help. Now I must dash and get those wages.'

This is a little illustration of how basic coaching techniques can turn an ugly confrontation into a productive conversation.

Now, you're not going to be a pest, forever scanning the airwaves for opportunities to coach whether it's welcome or not. You're a manager with your own accountabilities, not a professional coach. Sometimes you'll have to do a fair bit of it, other times not so much. People differ in temperament and circumstance. Jane might enter a white-water patch with the RFI issue and need a series of quick coaching conversations over the period to navigate it. Other times, she's plugging away, happy and independent. It will be the same for all members of your team.

If you think that adopting a coaching style of management means you'll be having more conversations with your people than you did before, you may be right. That's the whole point: to activate you as the manager your people need. It requires an upfront investment of your time, but consider what you get in return. You know what's really going on with the project and the team. The opportunities to articulate your expectations with regard to the results you're all striving for multiply. People are giving their all because they feel supported, valued, and that you really care about them and the result. As you coach them and they coach each other and even – why not? – you, the chemistry of good productivity spreads. People are pulling together to realise a clearly defined common goal. Everyone trusts each other to do the right thing in support of that goal. They are talking to each other frankly and honestly, so that information flows to where it's needed, when it's needed. Everyone is on high alert for anything that might jeopardise the result and they take timely and concerted effort to eliminate the risk. There is an *esprit de corps* of learning lessons and moving forward briskly; no one's that interested in blame and recrimination. So yes, it requires an upfront investment of your time, but think of the stress, waste, loss and slog caused by bad chemistry that you're avoiding. It's a sound investment.

CHAPTER 10

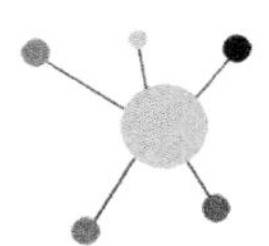

Managing your own state: How to be when you coach

We venture a little further into coaching territory now because we need to talk about 'self as instrument'. You become an instrument when you coach, one designed to enable enhanced thinking in the thinker. You can't be an effective instrument if you're not in the right state. Your state, who and what you are in that moment, is more important than what you do or say.

Coaching is an intervention, and the success of any intervention depends on the inner state of the intervener, more than the strategies, tools or techniques the intervenor uses.[1] In a football match, if you're a defender and you tackle an attacker, you've made an intervention. Now imagine you've just had a hairdryer thrown at you by your furious

---

[1] For more on this, see *Presence: Exploring Profound Change in People, Organizations and Society*, by Peter Senge et. al.

manager in the half-time talk, and inside you're knotted up, seething, feeling bullied, angry and indignant. You return to the pitch and in the first five minutes you vexatiously take out an opponent, causing a career threatening injury for them, yourself to be sent off and your team to lose. It was a bad intervention because your state was a mess. Note that football star Gary Lineker never got a yellow or red card once in his sixteen-year career.[2] That's an inner state!

Your state matters, too. If you've got a day of back-to-back meetings, you'll probably be frazzled well before the end. After such a dump of input, impressions, information, ideas and things to remember and do, you can't think straight. That's your state. When an event you've planned starts with mishaps and emergencies, leaving you stressed and frantic, that's your state and it rubs off on others. When you coach, you need to be grounded and centred. You have to listen, notice what's going on, and reflect back to the thinker. It's hard to do that if you're full of anxiety, frustration and racing thoughts. You need to be 'on purpose', which means you are crystal clear on the purpose of the intervention, and how it sits within the broader purpose that drives the team. You are calm, resolute, supple and ready for whatever happens.

To say it again, this is far more important than the

---

[2] James Dart, 'Multi-talented footballers', *The Guardian*, 10 August 2005: https://www.theguardian.com/football/2005/aug/10/theknowledge.sport

strategies, tools or techniques you use. It took me quite a few years to get this as a coach. I would search for thrilling activities to put my clients through, scour books for a brilliant passage to impress them with, and spend hours composing the 'killer' question that would knock their socks off. I still do that a bit, but now I spend more time on my inner state so I can be present with the thinker without distracting them from their thinking.

People compose themselves in different ways. They go for a walk, or a bike ride, or talk things through with someone. When I don't have time for that, I do a physical exercise, which I'll share with you here in case it's useful.

Plant your feet hips-width apart, your weight evenly distributed. Feel the ground beneath your feet. Then, gently unlock your knees. Imagine there is a string coming out of the top of your head that is pulling you upward. Place your hands on your stomach. This is your centre of gravity, where your gravitas comes from. Breathe in for three seconds and out for five. In for three, out for five. Feel your back. Imagine all your knowledge, all your experience, all your relationships, all your support – right behind you, at your back, right now. Lean gently into it. Feel that support. Now lean forward slightly from the chest. That's your future. Lean into your future. Then sway gently back and forth to find your middle point. This is you, grounded, supported by the ground, and centred in the present and in your gravitas. You're balanced between your back, your history, and your front, the future. You're calm, grounded and centred, ready to be an instrument.

But first you need to calibrate yourself as a coaching instrument. Before I coach, I go through a checklist to remind myself of what we're here to do. The coaching conversation is not about me, it's about the thinker. Ethically, everything that's said in the coaching conversation is confidential. My job is to establish a safe space and process to enable the thinker's thinking. They do the work. I notice, rather than diagnose. I maintain a respectful distance as a thinking partner. Coaching doesn't work when the coach tries too hard or gets too close. Trust the coaching process more than you trust yourself as a coach at any given time. Let go of the need to control and the need to be right. The thinker in front of me is robust and able to sort their own stuff out. If they're genuinely not, then coaching is not for them. My role is to facilitate the process. I don't get involved in the thinker's content because that belongs to them.

So, to recap, before you make a coaching intervention, check your state, get grounded and centred, and calibrate. When you've decided that the next ten, twenty, forty minutes with your colleague is going to be coaching, check the boss – you – at the door and retool yourself as an instrument of their thinking for the coming moments.

CHAPTER 11

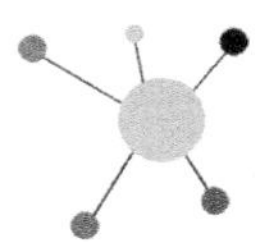

Coaching for curmudgeons: Check your mindset

I hope you'll agree that the techniques I've set out here are not difficult. Most of us employ them without thinking in our dealings with the people we care about. The leap is to employ them in the management of others in our professional lives. We're allowed to do that, and it works. You can even do it if, temperamentally, you're a bit of a curmudgeon, i.e. tending toward bad temper and grumpiness. It should be clear by now that coaching is not being nice and smiley all the time. At root, it's about making yourself available to listen and to appreciate your people. 'Appreciate' here has a double meaning. It is both acknowledging the value of your people, and also increasing the value of your people by helping them grow in capability and confidence. Even curmudgeons can do that.

That said, there are some attitudes and habits of mind – what we call 'mindset' – that will help you coach more effectively if you cultivate them in yourself. Three things in particular curmudgeons need to do: 1) value progress over perfection; 2) cultivate a growth mindset; and 3) put your trust in trustworthiness. Let's look at each of them in turn.

Give progress its due

Say we're standing on a beach on a clear, sunny day, looking out over the calm water. What do we see? We see the horizon. But is the horizon actually there? It looks like the point where the sky meets the sea, but no such point exists in reality. It's something conceived in our heads to make sense of an optical illusion.[1]

Something similar happens when we set targets, such as for the completion of a project. The target becomes a vision of perfection, something we can picture vividly even though it doesn't exist yet. The distance between where we are and the realisation of the vision is the distance left to go, and it can get us down. Sometimes we can be so oppressed by the distance separating us from the vision that we ignore the progress we've made toward it. It's important because if you always measure your progress against the vision, you'll always fall short and be disappointed. But if you measure progress against where you started, you will definitely have

1 For this insight I'm grateful to Dan Sullivan, founder of the Strategic Coach Program.

made progress and you can feel good about that.

In coaching, you need to give progress its due, and not let perfection oppress you both and erode your confidence. Hold in your mind the idea that if we keep making progress, we'll get there. If we fret too much about the distance to go, we'll always feel like we're failing. This stifles the thinker's ability to think and act. Who would you prefer to work for, a boss who measures your progress exclusively against the vision, and forever finds you falling short, or a boss who measures your progress against where you started, and appreciates your progress?

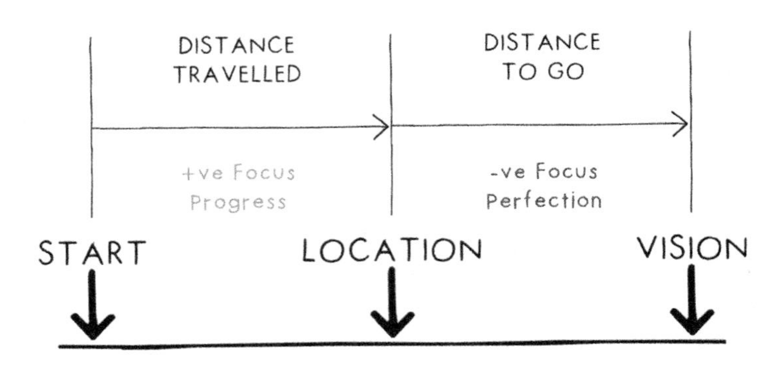

Figure 4. Progress vs Perfection. Measure and celebrate progress because, if we fret too much about the distance to go, we'll always feel like we're failing.
(Credit: Dave Stitt)

This is quite a controversial idea for construction because we have hard deadlines to meet. People I coach say, 'No, Dave, this is a recipe for complacency. We have targets for a reason.' And I agree. We have to set targets, and they have to be stiff. But setting targets and measuring progress are two separate conversations. When I work with executive teams aiming for a big vision, we glance up at it to orient ourselves but we don't dwell on the distance to go. Instead, we maintain our focus on the intermediate milestones directly ahead, and measure progress against where we started. Valuing progress instead of perfection builds confidence, which boosts our energy, stimulates lateral thinking, and helps us take necessary risks. If you are constantly reminding the thinker of the distance between here and perfection, and letting them know how much it bothers you, they will be less confident and less capable.

So, celebrate progress deliberately and regularly. If we're not in the habit of celebrating progress, the progress we're making may not be apparent to us. Take some time to think about the progress your team has made. Be specific: compose a statement that quantifies the progress and praises the people and actions that made it happen. Then say it.

Cultivate a growth mindset

In her book on the topic, Stanford University psychology professor Carol Dweck distinguishes between a growth mindset and a fixed mindset. A person with a fixed mindset believes their talent is innate, that they were born with it, that it's a fixed quantity and cannot be increased. Failure is a disaster for them because it's a reflection on their whole selves. Studies show that fixed-minded people habitually avoid difficulty, so as not to be exposed (in their minds) as deficient. They want to be the best, so they avoid obstacles and difficulties. They see things in black and white, and people as either good or bad. They favour categorical statements like, 'It can't be done', and 'You just can't get the staff these days'.

On the other hand, people with growth mindsets believe talent can be acquired, and work hard to develop their potential. They're not bothered about being the best; they want to get better. They embrace obstacles and difficulties for the challenge of it because, for them, failure isn't disaster. It's success but not quite yet. And if someone insists something can't be done, they start looking for ways to do it.

The good news about mindsets is that they're not genetic. They're habits of thought, and you can change them. Depending on the day and how I'm feeling, I'm sometimes in growth mode and sometimes in fixed mode. If you're reading this, I expect you tend toward a growth mindset because you're curious about what I have to say in case it's useful. Someone with a fixed mindset is likely to think of themselves as knowing all there is to know about management already and that, anyway, you're either good at it or rubbish and that's that.

To adopt a coaching style of management, a growth mindset will really help. Without a growth mindset, you won't believe the thinker can ever overcome their barriers and improve. And you'll be too scared of failing to try coaching techniques. At the first difficulty, you'll say, 'See, I knew this would never work!'

Put your trust in trustworthiness

If you're going to bother to coach somebody, you have to have a certain level of trust in them because, otherwise, you'll judge it to be a waste of your time and effort. This can make coaching tricky because command-and-control managers in construction tend to feel that no one is as competent as they are, that no one cares as much as they do or works as hard. It's a by-product of the command-and-control culture. A common complaint, for instance, is that graduates arrive with their heads stuffed with ideas but no practical experience.

Sometimes the reasons a manager gives for the mistrust they feel can seem understandable but, in my experience, this kind of pessimism can also be reflexive, an excuse for managers to protect their status and power by hoarding accountability. I don't encourage managers to have blind faith in people, but I do encourage them to challenge their pessimism by making a more objective assessment of their people's trustworthiness.

I'm helped here by the philosopher Onora O'Neill, who has spent years examining the issue of trust and who put forward three criteria for assessing trustworthiness: competence, honesty and reliability. This is a good matrix. A chef may be competent to the point of giftedness and will never tell a lie but if, during a pre-theatre surge, he is found passed out in the wine cellar, he is unreliable, and the owner will be justified in letting him go. Similarly, a sales manager may be great at the job and deliver consistent results, all while merrily siphoning 5% of your profits off into a secret account in Panama. He is reliable and competent, but dishonest. And in choosing between two accountants to look after my tax affairs, each honest and reliable, should I choose the one just out of university, or the one with ten years' experience in my type of business? Clearly, the latter is likely to be more competent.

To O'Neill's three criteria I will add a fourth – caring – an attribute that encompasses empathy, commitment and a willingness to help. I use these four criteria in a tool called the Trustworthy Tracker, which should help you make an evidence-based assessment of a person's trustworthiness.[2]

---

[2] I developed the Trustworthy Tracker for my 2018 book, *Deep and Deliberate Delegation: A New Art for Unleashing Talent and Winning Back Time*. You can download a printable version of the Tracker free of charge here: https://dsabuilding.co.uk/daily_tip/how-to-trust-those-around-you/

	CARING	HONEST	RELIABLE	COMPETENT
LEVEL 5	They seem to have an innate sense for my needs and interests and, without prompting, work towards an outcome that is win-win for both of us 3	They tell the truth regardless of self-interest; I always get the full picture 3	They consistently do what they say they'll do; my commitments are safe with them 3	They exhibit mastery by anticipating what needs to be done in any situation and knowing how to do it intuitively 5
LEVEL 4	They ask about my needs and interests and will generally take opportunities, when they crop up, to realise common goals 2	I feel confident thy are telling the truth because I have checked on a number of occasions 2	They mostly do what they say, and let me know in advance if they need more time or help 2	They are expert, responding quickly to a manifest need through a mix of reasoning and some intuition, drawing on a repertoire of rules-based approaches 4
LEVEL 3	When specifically asked, they will make some effort to accommodate my needs and interests 1	Sometimes I have to ask questions to get the full picture 1	In the end the task gets done, though sometimes after a reminder, and/or sometimes late 1	They are proficient, showing good familiarity with the rules, which allows them to calculate a dependable response across most situations 3
LEVEL 2	They are sometimes not receptive to requests for cooperation 0	Often what they tell me doesn't feel right, or quite match other accounts 0	If I don't hassle them it doesn't get done 0	As an experienced beginner, they follow rules and instructions and show some ability to adapt to unexpected situations 2
LEVEL 1	Intentionally or not, they sometimes seem to work against my interests 0	It's clear to me they are obfuscating and deflecting to protect their self-interest 0	They never deliver and are immune to pleas and threats 0	A novice, they laboriously follow rules, and are flummoxed when there is no obvious application of them 1

'The Trustworthy Tracker' (© Dave Stitt 2013)

Figure 5. Use the Trustworthy Tracker to score a person's trustworthiness.

To use the Trustworthy Tracker, score the person on each of the four criteria using the Tracker as a guide. This will give you four numbers, which you multiply together for the score. On a piece of paper, it would look like this:

Caring [score] x Honest [score] x Reliable [score]
x Competent [score] = total score

Let's say a person is super impressive, and gets all Level Five scores. They would get the maximum 135 points:

Caring [3] x Honest [3] x Reliable [3] x Competent [5] = 135

Clearly, you can trust this person, maybe more than you thought before. However, notice that the scoring scheme drops steeply. If they score consistently on the next level down, they would receive thirty-two points, as follows:

Caring [2] x Honest [2] x Reliable [2] x Competent [4] = 32

And if they are consistently mediocre, they get only three points:

Caring [1] x Honest [1] x Reliable [1] x Competent [3] = 3

The reason for this is that Caring, Honest and Reliable are intimately bound up with trust, a delicate and precarious thing, so much so that if candidates score in the bottom two levels of these criteria, their score, unfortunately, is zero. More likely, the person will zigzag up and down among the top three levels to get a score in the thirties or above, what I call the Zone of Potential. That means they'll have strengths you can build on, and areas in which they might profit from some targeted support.

This is a blunt tool, but it's better than unchallenged, reflexive pessimism, which will stifle your team and hold it back.

Now that we've gone through the basics of a coaching approach to management, I'd like to zoom back out and take a more analytical look at why construction needs this. In Chapter 2, I explained why your company needs this from the viewpoint of culture, people and productivity. In the next chapter, I will analyse why construction projects in particular need a coaching approach, given their nature.

CHAPTER 12

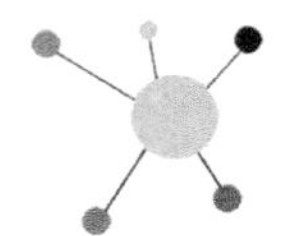

Construction projects and the never-ending fight against entropy

I see coaching as a social technology – an app, if you like – that is better suited to the construction industry as it has evolved to this point in time. In particular, it is better suited than the command-and-control style of management that still dominates. Let's look now at why this is from the perspective of the construction project itself, which is what the construction business is all about.

A construction project is complex, not complicated. The two words are often used interchangeably, but there is an important difference. A Swiss watch is complicated. Take the back off one and you will see an amazing feat of engineering. All those tiny springs, cogs and levers operating perfectly in unison to tell time with near absolute precision over many years. The challenge of fitting all that know-how and capability into such a small space will have seemed impossible centuries ago to watchmakers, but it is possible, and the techniques for doing it are known and repeatable. The problem is complicated, but it has been solved.

Complex problems are different. They have yet to be solved. They have multiple causes and moving parts, over which no one has total command. The physical, political and social contexts of a complex problem are in flux. The actors involved have competing, evolving agendas. The system of a complex problem is non-linear, meaning there is often no direct correlation between what you do to it (inputs) and what comes out the other end (outputs).[1] Unlike a Swiss watch, nothing quite like it has ever occurred before.

On paper, a new hospital is complicated, like a Swiss watch. Its structure, plant, machinery and technology have all been worked out. In lab conditions, building it would be straightforward. But here's the twist: hospitals are not built in lab conditions. They are built by teams of strangers, often with competing agendas, answerable to multiple stakeholders in challenging logistical conditions, with weather and other unpredictable constraints thrown into the mix. That makes it a system of systems, and it is complex.

We put our faith in the hard systems set up to control the outcome: contracts, the programme, project management

---

1 I'm guided here by a paper by Dr. Sholom Glouberman and Dr. Brenda Zimmerman, entitled 'Complicated and Complex Systems: What Would Successful Reform of Medicare Look Like?', Discussion Paper No. 8, Commission on the Future of Health Care in Canada, July 2002. Available at: http://publications.gc.ca/site/eng/235920/publication.html

protocols and software. They should keep everybody on track, but we know they don't. Hard systems and a command-and-control management culture are not sufficient to solve the complex problem of a major construction project for two reasons. The first is that command-and-control suppresses the knowledge and initiative lying latent in your team; they will be waiting for you to perceive the problem and issue orders accordingly, and you may not do that in time, and your orders may not be correct because you're not omniscient. The second reason is that relationships wither in conditions where command-and-control management tries to enforce hard systems; as I've set out above, relationships are the foundation of results.

Command-and-control's vulnerability is explained by the second law of thermodynamics, which states that in a closed system, entropy – which means disorder – always increases. Usable energy is forever dissipating in search of equilibrium, and the state of perfect equilibrium is perfect uselessness. This happens in organisations, as well, including those involved in the construction of hospitals. Energy always dissipates. The focus, determination and drive that manifested at the start of the project won't be maintained without effort. People naturally creep into comfort zones, sink into routine and compare what needs to be done against the wording of their job descriptions.

Fortunately, however, companies and projects are not closed systems. Energy can be injected from outside or mustered from within to do new, useful things. Project leaders have to do this all the time. They must be restless, activist busybodies, spotting opportunities and risks the second they appear on the horizon, and mustering the collective energy needed to seize the opportunities and neutralise the risks. Entropy is construction's enemy; it makes us roll over to risk.

Risk comes in many forms. It could be error visible to the eye, but it could also be something more intangible: the growth of a culture in which error can breed; conflict; negligent attitudes or behaviour; the onset of substandard outcomes; signs of actors scuttling into positions of selfish risk aversion (think of Jane and her RFI). When they spot this, project leaders must respond skilfully, imaginatively, thinking outside the box. They must launch projects within the project to keep the project on track. But they can't do this all by themselves. They need skilful, imaginative and willing help – practical help and thinking help – from the talented people in their team. A manager who has cultivated a culture in which people are activated by coaching will find it far easier to muster the energy in the team that is needed to do the new, useful things that project success depends on. A coaching management culture will open a new front against our great enemy, entropy.

PART THREE

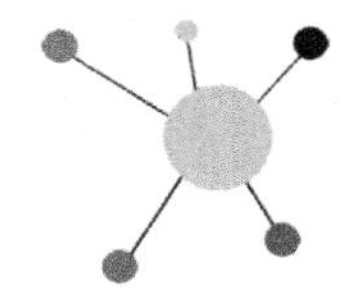

Changing the Industry From the Ground Up

CHAPTER 13

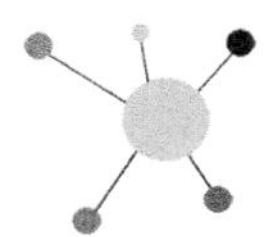

Why am I doing this?

After fifteen years of cutting my teeth, getting qualified and moving up the ladder in Taylor Woodrow, I was headhunted by Birse Construction in 1991 to be a senior project manager. Younger folks may not be familiar with the legendary Birse Group, which was bought and absorbed by Balfour Beatty in 2014. In the early 1990s it was rarely out of the news for conflicts with clients. It had an aggressive, winner-take-all culture. In 1997 the founder, Peter Birse, took the unprecedented step of making a public apology for the company's behaviour earlier in the decade.

Joining Birse in 1991 was a culture shock. On the first day, one of my bosses said, 'I'm going to tell you what to do, and if you don't do it, there'll be bust ups.' Another said, 'We'll soon see what you're made of.' When I asked for my Birse tie, my boss growled, 'We don't do them.' When I asked for the Birse procedures manual, he growled, 'We don't do them either, just get on with it!' It was like the Wild West after the civility and decorum of my Taylor Woodrow family.

I was told that if you can hack it at Birse you can hack it anywhere, and I believed it; they were hard on their clients, hard on their subcontractors and even harder on their staff. But at the time I found it incredibly exciting. The company was growing fast, and always trying new approaches and quickly ditching most in a frantic attempt to find out what worked.

By the mid 90s, however, it was suffering serious growing pains and two external coaches were brought in to initiate what was called the Birse Transformation Programme. Somehow – fate, perhaps – I found myself drawn in, joining the first cohort of the seven-day Intensive Programme, and then the internal Coaching the Coaches programme to train ten people, including me, to be internal coaches with the aim of keeping the transformation going after the external coaches had left.

This changed my life. It changed Birse, too. By then, I was on a divisional business board and on it, I experienced energy and team working like never before and seldom since.

I became less interested in bricks and blocks and concrete and more interested in people, particularly teams. Up to that point, my twenty-year career in construction had been a hard fight with just about everybody: subcontractors, designers, clients and at times my fellow workers, staff and bosses. Initially, I thought it was just me, although, as I matured, I started to see that this is how the industry was. But now I had discovered a new way: a coaching style of relating to people, doing business and getting stuff done.

In 1998 I was headhunted again and joined Wates Construction in an operations management role. Around that time, Wates was seeking culture change as well, and so, owing to my experience with Birse, I was soon leading Wates' transformation programme, called Improving Construction. And as part of that programme I co-led the Wates Coaching the Coaches programme to train forty staff as internal coaches and facilitators to roll out the transformation. It was a success. It won awards and, looking back in 2020, Wates Group chairman Sir James Wates said the programme 'yielded excellent results and contributed to building a foundation for significant growth of the Wates Group in subsequent years'. Thanks, Sir James!

In summer 2001, I left Wates to set up my own company, DSA Building Performance Ltd., to coach construction company boards and project leadership teams. The day I set up DSA, I declared to myself and those around me that my mission was to change the construction industry. I believed I had discovered a better way of doing the construction business – a way in which people can thrive and get things built well, working collaboratively.

One of my first big clients was Costain. In the late 1990s,

Costain was in trouble. Trading in its shares was suspended in 1996 after two profit warnings. In 2001 the then chief executive Stuart Doherty and systems director Mark Bew initiated a change programme called Implementing Best Practice (IBP). DSA was invited to design and facilitate the IBP programme to all Costain staff, which involved 10,000 person-days of training between 2002 and 2008.

It was a dramatic turn-around programme for the entire UK contracting business, leading to a new pattern of business success, with Costain getting the *New Civil Engineer* Contractor of the Decade Award in 2010. In 2014, Tony Blanch, then Costain's group business improvement director, said: 'This had a significant impact on Costain's performance, creating One Costain and the stable foundation and springboard to our success.' Thanks, Tony!

There have been many other successes along the way, big and small, but in 2020 I looked at myself in the mirror and realised that while I was helping individual people, companies and projects, this wasn't having any impact at all on the culture of construction, which was still taking its toll on people, companies and clients. I reckoned that, at the rate I was going, it would take around 900 more years to make any impression on the industry. That's when I conceived my big idea: train thousands of young professionals in the essentials of a coaching management style so they become better managers – in the process changing the industry's culture from the inside out and from the ground up.

Am I being naïve again, like I was in asking for the company manual at Birse? Maybe, but in the next chapter I'll explain why I think this kind of industry change is possible.

CHAPTER 14

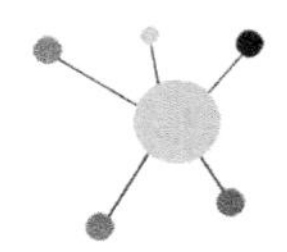

How an industry can change

How do you shift an ideology that has dominated a culture for centuries? That was the question posed by the RSA's Anthony Painter in a March 2021 article exploring how humanity could move forward more collaboratively in the age of pandemics. His answer was: alternative action at scale and over time.[1] One needs to correct, correct and correct again until the new way of thinking has replaced the old. The ideology he wanted to see replaced was the notion that struggle among humans for domination was just part of the natural order of things. Better and more sensible, to him, was the idea that everybody wins with true cooperation.

I believe that the same approach – alternative action at scale and over time – can be employed to replace the

---

1 Anthony Painter, 'See the future. Act now', RSA Blog, 4 March 2021. https://www.thersa.org/blog/2021/03/see-the-future-act-now

dominant command-and-control management culture in construction with a coaching management culture, which, as I hope I've adequately demonstrated, is a social technology-update construction sorely needs.

If I had the opportunity once again to lead big culture-change programmes at Birse, Wates and Costain, knowing what I know now, I would make the dissemination of basic coaching techniques among managers central to the effort. Back then, our approach was to try and shift people's attitudes, to get them to see the benefit of new ways of doing business. Changing attitudes is a difficult thing to do, because it means tampering with a person's personality and sense of self, which people naturally resist. Coaching is a technique more than it is an attitude, and people are far more willing to adopt techniques than shift their attitudes, especially if the techniques work. Creating a growing body of coach-managers, as we're setting out to do now, would have made change happen faster, go deeper and be more permanent.

In the effort to replace construction's command-and-control management culture with a coaching one, we have a powerful ally in the natural contagiousness of human behaviour. We are intensely social mammals, and the compulsion to mimic each other's moods and behaviours, consciously and unconsciously, is wired into our physiology. When we admire someone else's dance move, we're likely to experience heightened neuron activity in the matching parts of our own body. Controlled studies have shown that people in groups with positive and energetic leaders become positive and energetic, while those in groups with negative and low-energy leaders become correspondingly dreary. 'People are sort of walking mood conductors and we need to be aware of that,' said University of Pennsylvania professor Sigal Barsade, who conducted the research.[2]

This means that a coaching style of management, which involves both mood and behaviour, is a strong candidate for exponential growth in the construction industry. The power of exponential growth should be clear to us from the coronavirus pandemic, which saw much of the world locked down just a few months after the first case of Covid-19 was identified in Wuhan. Back in 1969, physics professor Albert A. Bartlett said: 'The greatest shortcoming of the human race is our inability to understand the exponential function.'[3] Fifty-two years on, I'm not sure we've got it yet.

It won't happen on its own, otherwise I wouldn't have needed to develop the Coach for Results course, or write this book. If a coaching style of management is supported by company bosses, and practised by managers, I believe the natural contagiousness of human behaviour will make it spread in organisations, especially if we talk about what

---

2 For an accessible round-up of research into this topic, see 'Contagious Behavior', by Shirley Wang, published 1 February 2006 on the website of the Association Psychological Science. https://www.psychologicalscience.org/observer/contagious-behavior

3 Albert A. Bartlett, 'Arithmetic, population and energy', lecture at University of Colorado Boulder, 19 September 1969.

we're doing and why we're doing it. But we have to prime the pump. Currently, the 'R' number for command-and-control (meaning its reproduction rate thanks to behavioural contagiousness) is higher than the 'R' number for a coaching style of management. However, by training thousands of young construction professionals in the essentials of coaching, we can interrupt their slide into command-and-control and divert their trajectory towards coaching. As older managers retire, the balance could tip. This is alternative action at scale and over time.

The coaching style of management is seeded in a team or organisation . . .

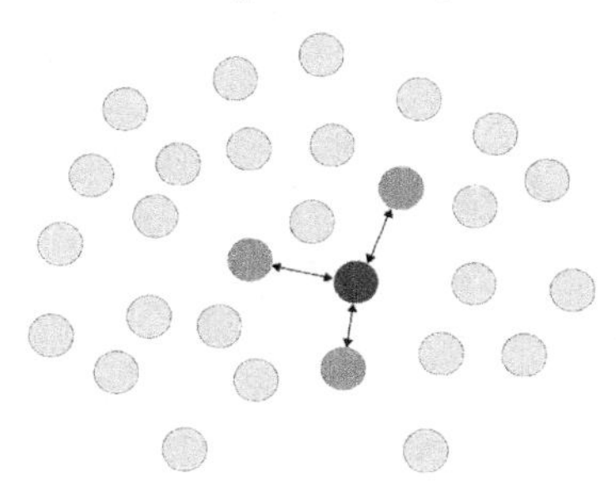

. . . that is disparate, siloed and thus suboptimally productive.

It spreads . . .

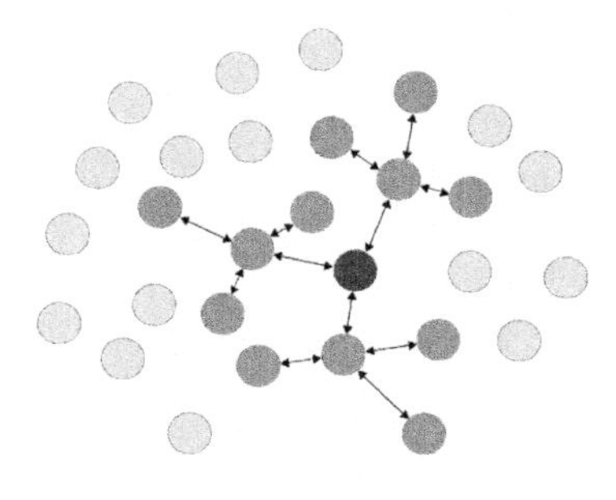

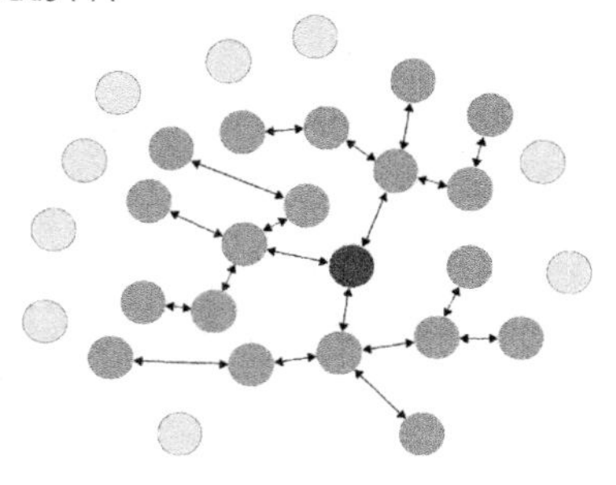

and spreads . . .

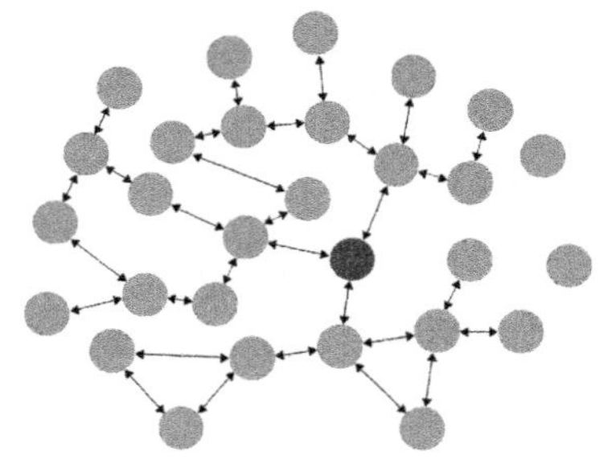

. . . until the team is engaged, activated
and pulling together powerfully.

Figure 6. How coaching spreads in an organisation. (Credit: Rod Sweet)

CHAPTER 15

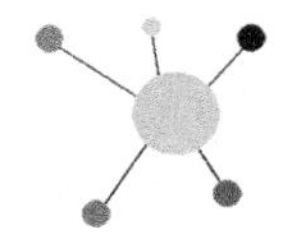

How will you lead the way?

You're nearly finished reading this book and maybe you've also completed the Coach for Results course. Congratulations! You could be a pioneer in construction's new management paradigm.

Maybe you've already begun working on your coaching management style. If so, what are you noticing? Is it showing up in the results you are achieving? Or if you haven't dipped your foot into the coaching water yet, how are you going to start? Will you tell people around you that you're trying out a different way of getting things done, that you're a student of a coaching style of management, that you may make mistakes, learn from them and try again? I hope you do, because that will intrigue people and assist the spread of the technique. Or will you try coaching by stealth, and just get on with it as naturally as you can? You decide what's best for you, what you are comfortable with or not. Chances are it's not going to be plain sailing and you see it as an opportunity to get out of your comfort zone and learn.

Throughout this book I've said the basic coaching techniques are easy to do, and they are, but I'll say again that mastering them in the real world is not. That's because when you coach, you're coaching into a living, complex system. The thinker is a living, complex system embedded in other living, complex systems, and the effects are not always predictable. And you are similarly complex, emotional and not as rational as you might like to think you are. So, it may be a bumpy ride to begin with.

In her book, *Nine Things Successful People Do Differently*, Heidi Grant Halvorson explains how those going into a challenge thinking it'll be easy often find it extremely discouraging when they encounter the first obstacle, whereas realistic optimists know it's going to be a challenge, so they work on making success happen through planning, persistence and choosing the right strategies. That sounds sensible to me.

Have a go, get started and be confident that a) it will work for you and that b) you're part of construction's new and better future.

To learn more about the Coach for Results course, visit https://dsabuilding.co.uk/#coach4results

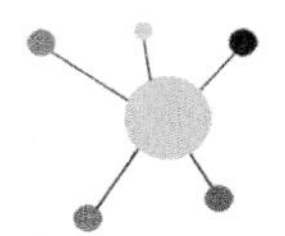

Acknowledgements

The Coach for Results course and book would not have been possible without the assistance of my son Greg Stitt, illustrator Gary Nightingale, and editor Rod Sweet. Also, thanks to Claire Pedrick, of 3D Coaching, my mentor coach, and whose book, *Simplifying Coaching*, exerted a strong influence on this book. I owe a special thanks to Sue for her limitless love, encouragement and support.

Printed in Great Britain
by Amazon